SHE BEAT THAT GOOSE TO DEATH

STORIES OF NAN PATTON

SHE BEAT THAT GOOSE TO DEATH

STORIES OF NAN PATTON

EDITED AND COMPILED BY ANN WHITFORD

www.bookstandpublishing.com

Published by
Bookstand Publishing
Morgan Hill, CA
Record 4188_4

ISBN 978-1-61863-943-1

Printed in the United States of America

iv

PREFACE

If you are holding this book in your hands right now, you probably knew Nan. So the stories you find here are ones you may have already heard. You will probably be able to picture her telling them…maybe even hear her words in your head as you read. This book is a poor substitute for her much perfected delivery, stand-up (and sometimes sit-down) comic that she was, but it will have to do.

Because so many people contributed to this book, you may discover some things about Nan that you didn't know. I'm sure there are other stories out there, too, and I regret not being able to find them all.

If you didn't know Nan….well, you sure missed a special person. I hope this book gives you a sense of who she was, and how she touched so many people

Nan always wanted to write a book. She had the title picked out, "She Beat That Goose to Death", so that's the title I used. It's a follow-up to her grandmother's books, "I'll Gather My Geese" and "My Goose Is Cooked".

People who knew Hallie Stillwell, her grandmother, often said that Nan was a chip off the old block…very much like Hallie and Nan's mother, Dadie. That pleased Nan, who always insisted that she (Nan) was Hallie's favorite granddaughter. Nan's style was strictly her own, though, falling more in the category of pure entertainment with perhaps a bit of history alongside, while Hallie's leaned heavily into the historical, philosophical realm. Nan's sense of humor was legendary, and an integral part of her storytelling. Her quick wit and great timing served her well, both in telling stories and just in everyday conversation. To be around Nan was fun. She reveled in keeping everyone amused, and there was never a dull moment when you were with her.

Whenever Nan discussed writing her book, she was somewhat reluctant to start, stating that she couldn't write as well as she could tell stories. But together we figured out that she could write them down as close as possible to the way she recited them, and I could then edit them. Of course, in the simple reading of her stories, you miss her wonderful facial expressions, gestures, and dramatic pauses, etc., but we did the best we could. Those extra visual and auditory tidbits, you just have to fill in with your imagination.

When we finally got going on her book project, little did we both know that she had so little time left. She had just started writing her stories when she began to have some strange speech symptoms. It took almost a year for the medical experts to discover that those symptoms were the early stages of bulbar palsy, a progressive and fatal disease. When she was finally told what it was, and that it was terminal, she knew she didn't have much time left. That spurred her to get as much done as she could, but the disease was swift in its progression. Too soon, she ran out of energy and the physical strength to even write. But I assured her that I'd make sure the book was finished, and include all of her stories and more.

After we lost Nan, in July of 2012, Kay, her oldest sister, helped continue work on the book. She gave me more names of people to contact who had known Nan. She excitedly anticipated seeing it in print. I am so disappointed that she did not live to see the final product. Her sudden passing in October 2013 was another cruel blow to those of us who loved them both. Kay was my expected source for the biographical details of Nan's life.

So instead, I turned to Fred, Nan's son, to fill in as much as possible. Most of the information in the biographical section came from Fred, and I thank him for his time searching his memory for the parts of Nan's life prior to the time most of us knew her at "the ranch".

Nan's many, many friends also submitted stories, memories, photos, and tributes to Nan, which help to tell who she is…an important aspect of Nan's story. Thanks to all of them for their input and assistance.

I only knew Nan for a few years, though the time spent with her was considerable during the winters we stayed at Stillwells. She had so many plans for the future and it is truly tragic that she wasn't able to see them all realized.

But here is her book! And that was a very important item on her bucket list.

This book has been a labor of love, and it seems to have taken much longer than I anticipated. It was all for you, dear Nan. I hope you are pleased with the final result.

Ann Whitford
Summer 2014

**Nan stamping a signature in her grandmother's book,
"I'll Gather My Geese"**

ACKNOWLEDGEMENTS

To Barbara Fisher for transcribing her video of "Radioactive Nan".
To Betty Hamilton for proofreading and editing suggestions.
To Barbie Maher for supplying the video of "Retirement Stories".
To Fred Patton, who supplied details of his mom's life before her move "to the ranch".
To the late Kay Pizzini, who provided so much information and additional names of Nan's friends to contact.
To all the friends of Nan who contributed items to this book.
To others who encouraged me to complete it for her.

Photo credits to: Cindy Bolton, Darlene Boyer, Carol Dunn, Richard and Barbara Fisher, Bob Freeman, Bob Herr, David Moffitt, Fred and Robin Patton, Richard and Joan Payne, Sande Pedro, Tom Petit, Kay Pizzini, Cathy Ritter, Eldon Whitford, and Dutch Zondervan.

This book would not have been possible without all of your help.

INTRODUCTION

A BRIEF BIOGRAPHY OF MARIE NANNETTE PATTON

Marie Nannette Patton was born in Alpine, Texas, on July 19, 1949. She was several weeks premature, and had medical issues early on. At some point she was diagnosed with cerebral palsy, and had mobility issues throughout her life. One leg especially never "worked right" and she walked with a considerable limp.

Nan, as she came to be called, was born while her mother, Dadie, was attending college at Sul Ross in Alpine, and Nan's first few years were spent there in Alpine. Nan was the third child in the family, having two older sisters, Kay and Linda. Then her younger sister, Marlene was born, the last child from Dadie's marriage to Emeril Martin.

Dadie married W.T. Potter in Alpine. He had been born in Fort Worth, but was working for the REA, bringing electricity to the Big Bend area, when they met. He and Dadie had a son, Travis, born in 1955. Travis said Nan was his favorite sister, because she was the only one he could outrun!

In 1956, the family moved to San Antonio. Dadie taught physical education at Gardner Middle School in San Antonio. Nan and several of her siblings attended school there.

Nan graduated from high school in San Antonio, most likely from McArthur High School. She got married while still in high school to Fred Patton.

After high school, the couple moved to Arlington, Texas, where Fred went to school at the University of Texas in Arlington. According to her son, Nan may also have gone there as well. She got some nursing training somewhere, but did not complete the nursing program. They lived in an apartment in Arlington. Their son, Freddy, was born on April 2, 1970, at a hospital in Arlington.

In 1975, when Freddy was 5, his parents divorced. Nan and Freddy moved back to San Antonio, where they lived with Dadie for a year or so until they got their own apartment in a low income housing complex. Nan first worked as a secretary for the San Antonio Board of Realtors. Then in 1978, Nan got a job with the telephone company, then AT&T.

Fred remembers that housing complex, living there from age 6 until he was about 10. In the center of the complex was the playground, with trees and playground equipment. The apartments were arranged in concentric circles around that center area. He said he was always outside, doing "boy things". His mom's rules were 1) stay within the apartment complex, and 2) always be home by dark. Once in a while he'd get engrossed in play and not be home by dark. "I remember that Mom would come outside, in the center area where the playground was. She'd stomp her (good) foot on the sidewalk and yell, 'FREDDIEEEEE!'"

In 1980, they moved, renting a house owned by Dadie. Nan said that Fred grew up quickly, having to "be her legs" on many occasions. They would go to the mall, Nan with her list and money. She would take a seat somewhere in the middle, and send Freddy to the various stores to get the items on the list for her.

In 1985, AT&T broke up and the Texas part became Southwestern Bell. Some of the San Antonio offices were closed, and Nan's job there was one of those cut. She was given the option to move to Houston or Dallas to continue working for the telephone company. She chose Dallas because she had previously lived there. She knew some people there as well as the area.

So she moved to Dallas, and Freddy began his sophomore year of high school there. He graduated from San Houston High School in Arlington in 1988.

They had been living in a rented house there in Arlington. According to Fred, soon after he turned 18 and graduated, his mom said to him, "I'm moving to Dallas. Where are you going?"

Nan's version was slightly different. She said he'd already been talking that he wanted to get an apartment, perhaps moving in with his friend, Kevin.

She then moved to downtown Dallas, to a high-rise apartment complex across the street from work at Southwestern Bell. Fred did share an apartment with Kevin for about a year, but then moved back home. Since Nan's first apartment had only one bedroom, they got a two bedroom apartment in the same complex, and stayed for another year or two.

Then Nan rented a house with her friend from work, Marge, who also had a couple of kids who lived with them. Eventually, Nan and Marge each got a small rental house, fairly close to one another. They could still ride to work together.

Nan retired from Southwestern Bell in early 2004, after 25 years of work with the telephone company.

She then moved to "the ranch" in West Texas, the ranch that had been in the Stillwell family for decades, with its noted 4L brand. It is the site of "Hallie's Hall of Fame", the museum dedicated to the life of her grandmother, Hallie Crawford Stillwell. It also had an RV park and store. (Hallie's motto, printed on the t-shirts sold there: *Trust everybody but brand your cattle.*) Nan wanted to assist in the running of the family business and the museum.

She chose a plot of land from the ranch, fairly close to the store and museum, but with a view of Stillwell Mountain. Her longtime friend and on again/off again romantic partner, Larry Scoggins, built a house for her there. (Fred remembers him helping them move from Arlington to San Antonio when he was five.) He had also been an AT&T employee, working with Fred's dad there. Larry assisted with maintenance issues at the store and RV park. He lived there with her until 2011, a year before she passed, leaving soon after she received the devastating news about her terminal illness.

The store and RV park were open 7 days a week year round. The museum could be visited at any time. All you had to do was ask for the key at the store. Nan joined her step-father, W.T. Potter, in running the place. He had been in charge since the deaths of Hallie in 1997, followed by Nan's mother, Dadie, in 2000.

W.T. needed help and Nan was the perfect fit there, welcoming everyone with a smile, a kind word and, if you were lucky, a story or two.

Nan always loved the ranch. As a child, most vacations had been spent there, and it was always the hub of family get-togethers. Nan was proud of her Stillwell heritage, and loved being a part of the Stillwell Ranch RV Park and Store. She especially loved keeping the memory of her grandmother alive through the museum.

Nan would often have free programs in the evening at the museum, starting each program with stories about Hallie and the ranch, followed by showing the DVD, "Change in the Bend", which was primarily about the Stillwell family ranch and their neighbors.

Over the years, Nan's evening programs became a huge draw, especially for the winter snowbirds and tourists who came there, either to stay for the winter, or passing through on their way to Big Bend National Park. In 2005, music became a part of the programs, too, as "The Whitfords" performed from January through March. They always said they were a warm-up act for Nan, who told her own stories as well as those of her grandmother.

Nan always said her goal at Stillwells was to "make memories" for the campers and tourists. With her stories, the programs, music, dances, and campfires, as well as her delightful presence, she certainly did just that.

In 2010, Nan began having some unusual physical symptoms, including slightly slurred speech. She went from doctor to doctor to try to find out the cause. It wasn't until she went to the Mayo Clinic in Arizona in January of 2011 that she learned what was happening. She was diagnosed with bulbar palsy, a form of amyotrophic lateral sclerosis (ALS), often called Lou Gehrig's disease. Bulbar palsy begins in the neck/throat area, causing loss of speech and the ability to chew and swallow. It causes nerve and muscle deterioration that leads inevitably to death.

Nan stayed at the ranch, helping as much as she could for as long as she could. As her speech left her, she turned to a white board and marker, and communicated with that as well as with her wonderful smile and gestures. When she could no longer swallow, she had a feeding tube surgically implanted, and that gave her more time. Nan was used to dealing with adversity, and she fought to live as long as she could.

After celebrating her 63rd birthday at home on the ranch, she spent a few days in the Alpine hospital. She was then moved to the Odessa Home Hospice, where she passed just a few hours after arriving on July 26, 2012.

She was buried in the cemetery in Marathon, TX, with graveside services on Monday, July 30, 2012. The following February 2, a Celebration of Life was held in her honor at the Hallie Stillwell Hall of Fame, attended by her many friends and family members from all over Texas and the U.S.

Table of Contents

**Nan's usual spot for storytelling—
the piano bench in the museum**

Part I

Nan's Own Stories

Hallie's Hall of Fame Museum

1

THE DAY THE MUSEUM GOT ROBBED

I came to work at the store just as any other day. A couple came in to get the key for the museum. I gave the usual round of instructions: light switch on the right, the guest book on the left, movies to watch if they have time and be sure to turn off the lights, lock the door and return the key.

It wasn't long and they were back. They said, "We don't know if you know it or not, but the gun case is in the middle of the floor and there is nothing in it!"

Johnny went over and came back and said the museum had been robbed!

We called the sheriff's department and they came out and tried to find fingerprints. My point of view is they made such a mess doing that, but if they catch the thief, it will be worth it.

But the fingerprints and the rest of the investigation didn't solve the crime.

A couple of months after the break in, I was running the store by myself. At that time I was seldom left alone, but that day I was alone. I was sitting in the "Queen's" chair doing some quilting. The Queen's chair is where Hallie used to sit and greet people who would come to meet her.

I heard the bell on the store's door ring and got up to see who had come in. I was standing behind the counter and saw a man looking at Hallie's books. I said, "May I help you?"

He didn't turn around. So I said, "May I help you?" a little louder. I thought he might be hard of hearing.

Then he did turn around. He looked to be about 23 or 24 years of age.

He came up to the counter and said, "I'm the man that robbed the museum."

I plopped down on the stool and said "Oh." I thought to myself, "Did you forget something?"

He said, "When I was in the military I robbed a museum and they put me in the brig. While I was there, I tried to commit suicide and I almost succeeded. I want to commit suicide right now."

I sat there for what seemed like a long time, but probably it was only a few seconds. Then I said, "Do you have a family?"

He said, "I have a wife and a four-month-old baby." He brought out his wallet and showed me a picture of his baby.

I said, "That is a lot of pressure to put on a child, knowing his father committed suicide."

He said he had to come here to Stillwells to apologize and then his plan was to go to Terlingua, where he had committed another robbery, and apologize to them also.

He then told me his wife told him not to come, telling him, "You don't know what kind of people they are."

I told him it took a lot of courage for him to come in and apologize and that he had restored my faith in human nature. And to tell his wife he did the right thing.

As he stood there, he kept apologizing and we even both teared up a bit. I told him it wasn't my place to judge him and that everybody makes mistakes.

He told me how they did it. They came in through a window. That was a relief. I thought I had given them the key, since we always just handed it out to anyone who wanted to go to the museum.

He said at first he was only going to take the money out of the donation box. Then his partner said, "Let's take some of the cool stuff!"

They had parked two miles away and had to haul everything they stole to the car. They stole all the guns and artifacts out of the gun case, Hallie's arrowhead collection, and all the money out of the donation box.

I said, "We didn't even know how much money was in the donation box."

He said, "About one hundred fifty dollars", as he plopped a stack of twenties on the counter.

I was trying to decide what to do. Should I take the money? Should I not take the money? I wish someone would come in. Why isn't this guy in jail? All these things were going through my head. I made an executive decision and decided to keep the money.

I reached out and put my hand on the stack and was about to slide it across the counter when he said, "There is two hundred dollars there."

I said, "I have to give you change."

He said, "Keep the fifty dollars and put it toward a donation for the museum."

"I can't take more money than was taken," I replied. "You have that small baby at home and you will need the money."

So I gave him back the fifty extra dollars.

Well, you can only say "I'm sorry" and "I forgive you" so many times. I was wondering how many more times I was going to have to hear it when a customer came in.

By that time we were on a first name basis, so I said, "Hold on, Kirby."

As I looked at the most wonderful person I had ever seen come through the door, I said to her, "May I help you?"

Kirby turned around and said, "That's my mother."

I told her it took a lot of courage for her son to come in and apologize.

"He stole from you!" she exclaimed.

"He made a mistake," I responded. "Who hasn't made a mistake?"

They hung around for about thirty minutes. I tried to mosey them out the front door but as we got to the front porch, Kirby sat on a bench.

I sat down beside him and asked, "How old are you, Kirby?"

He said he just turned 35 on Monday. He and his mother finally left and I was feeling quite relieved.

Dad and Johnny came in for lunch and I was trying to tell them all the things that had happened. They were more interested in lunch than my story.

The only thing Johnny said was, "I wish I'd been here. I'd a kicked his ass!"

As I look back now, I think God must have had a hand in it. I was here by myself and usually I was never left at the store alone. Another odd thing is that no other customers came in during those two hours.

After Dad and Johnny ate, they went back on the ranch to finish the job they were doing.

A short time later, I was surprised to see Kirby and his mother come back in. He bought both of Hallie's books and two ice creams. He was going to give me that fifty dollars one way or another. I sold him the books and the ice cream. I figured he would have a lot of reading time on his hands.

Both of the robbers pleaded out and each got a sentence of 18 months. They did not go to trial.

We got everything back that had been stolen. It was an eye opener for us.

The next day I was in the Queen's chair again, and I couldn't stop thinking about the day before. I was worried about Kirby, and about his son growing up without a dad. I was worried about his future and his wife leaving him if he went to prison.

A voice said to me, "Nan, that was a test and you passed."

2

THE TWILIGHT ZONE

It was a long hot day. We had no business at all that day. Dad and I were wishing we would have at least one customer.

The phone rang. We rushed to answer it and for some reason I got to it before Dad.

The woman on the other end said that we had been recommended by the gas station attendant in Marathon. She wanted to know if we had hot water in our showers and if the bathrooms were heated. I told her we did and they were heated.

About an hour later, a woman drove up pulling a very old Airstream. I don't know anything about that kind of trailer, but it looked to me to be very old and I do think it had the original tires on it.

She came in the store and asked to see our bathrooms. I could hardly walk at that time because both my knees needed to be replaced. I hobbled out to the restroom at the end of the building to show her.

She walked in the bathroom and said, "There is no heat in here!"

There was a heat lamp in the ceiling, which I pointed out to her.

Then she said, "What is the closest spot to this bathroom that I can park in?"

I showed her the one closest to the restroom and she said that wasn't close enough.

Then she said that she would go instead to Study Butte and get a camping spot there. She asked me how long it would take her to get there. I said about two hours. Then she said it would not take that long. I thought, well, I live here and you don't. But I did not argue with her.

She and her friend left in a cloud of dust. I told Dad, "I'm glad they did not stay."

Some people you can't please, no matter how hard you try.

**Mary and her Airstream, back at Stillwells
a few years after the Twilight Zone Episode**

About 30 minutes later the phone rang. I answered it and the same woman was on the phone again. She said, "Don't ever recommend that Stillwell RV park again! It was like going into the Twilight Zone!"

She thought she had called the gas station. What she had done was hit redial and got Stillwell Store instead. I was very polite and said, "I sure won't!" and "Thanks for calling."

A couple years later, a woman named Mary started showing up at Stillwell's. She was quite friendly and came about twice a year. She also had an Airstream but it was a little newer. She was very helpful, like showing people where to park and being my legs so that I wouldn't have to walk so far.

One day I invited her to lunch. I was going to cook some stewed squash and she showed me that you didn't have to boil it in water the way my mother did. Just put some butter in the pan and it will make its own juice. It was the best squash I had ever eaten.

We were all sitting around the table enjoying our good fortune-- a wonderful meal and such good company, too. Who could ask for anything more?

I don't know if it was the lighting or the way she tilted her head. But it hit me! I said, "Are you the woman who came here a couple of years ago in an Airstream with a friend, then called back and said, 'Don't ever recommend this place. It is like going into the Twilight Zone'?"

"I was wondering how long it would take you to figure it out," she replied.

I finally got it. She has been a regular ever since.
We love Mary.

3

THE DAY MICHAEL CAME TO STILLWELL'S

One day I was at the store and a man came in and introduced himself. He said his name was Michael. He was a very quiet man and was living out in our primitive camping area.

Almost every day, he would walk in to the store and look for something to eat. I made some of my famous burritos and offered him one and he said, "I can't eat spicy food because of my stomach problems."

He slowly began to trust me and we started talking a little bit. I got the impression that he came out here to die. He had some kind of cancer and had walked out of the VA hospital, deciding that he didn't want any more treatments. He ended up at Stillwell's.

After about six weeks, he came in one day and asked about the little trailer we call Jack & Faye's trailer. It is about 1950's vintage. Very small and very cute. It had a bed, sink, stove and table. I told him it needed a lot of work. He asked me if he fixed it up, could he rent it? Of course I said yes.

During his stay here, I found out he was diabetic and was on insulin. I don't know how he kept his insulin cold when he was staying out in the primitive area. After he moved into the little trailer, he bought a small ice box and was quite happy in his new abode. True to his word, he was making improvements a little at a time on the trailer.

I hadn't seen Michael for about three days and I was going to check on him. But before I did, he came in the store and I was telling him how worried I had been about him. Then he told me what had happened to him.

He said he was under the trailer doing some minor repairs when he noticed he wasn't alone. He was in a very small space with a rattlesnake! He came out from under there as quickly as he could, but it was not quick enough. The snake made his strike and one of his fangs got caught in Michael's pant leg. He reached down and grabbed it by the head and wrung its neck.

So he had been bitten by a rattlesnake. He rolled up his pant leg to show me the fang marks.

I said, "Did you go to the hospital?" He said he hadn't.

I was trying to figure out how he managed that. I told him in the movies when someone got bit by a rattlesnake they always died. He let me stew on it awhile and then he told me it was a dry bite.

He said, "You know how you have an artificial knee?" He tapped on his knee and smiled. "I have one, too! That snake bit me on that knee and couldn't get through the titanium!"

He also told me he had skinned that snake and had it for supper. He had the last laugh on that snake.

Or maybe not, because he said that snake gave him a terrible bout of GAS.

4

A RAG QUILT STORY

The first rag quilt I ever made was beautiful. It was made out of flannel.

To make a rag quilt, you cut out a lot of squares and some half squares. You put them all together with the edges outside, and then you clip the seams. Every time you wash it, it frays a little more and that is why it is called a rag quilt.

I put it together and it was stunning. The colors were burgundy, gold, and greens.

Of course the first thing I wanted to do was sell it for a little extra spending money.

So, I took it to the local bank and showed the girls who work there my latest project. One of the girls was interested in buying it and asked how much I wanted for it. I had no idea.

I said, "What do you want to pay for it?"

She offered me $75 and I said how about $85. I walked out with $85 in my pocket. When I got home I was very proud of myself. If the truth be known, I probably spent more than $85 just on the material.

I made four more rag quilts in the next two years. Each one was prettier than the last. I learned a valuable lesson. I decided my time was worth something. I sold the next one for $100, the third one for $200, and the last one I made, I sold for $250.

On one of my trips to Alpine, I went to a restaurant to have lunch. The girl that bought my first quilt was in there with her family. She invited me to have lunch with them.

I was sitting by her mother and she asked me if I was still making rag quilts. I said yes. She wanted to know if I would do one for her and how much it would cost. I knew she probably knew how much her daughter had paid me for her quilt. I told her the last one I sold for $250, and of course I couldn't charge that much.

She said she wanted one of those $250 quilts. She pulled out her checkbook and wrote me a check for the whole amount. I told her that I wouldn't cash her check until the quilt was made.

I know me. In the past, I never know if I will get burned out. If that happens, there is no way I would finish that quilt. I was afraid that I would have spent the money and she would have no quilt. I held on to that check until the quilt was finished.

I finished the quilt and dropped it off. I went straight to the bank and cashed the check.

I was feeling pretty good. After all I had $250 in my purse. My hard work paid off. I was feeling good about myself. I was on my way home and was thinking of how I was going to spend my money.

I got as far as the Leary Ranch and the grass was high on the sides of the road. There in the high grass was a buzzard having lunch. I did not see him until he tried to take off. He was trying to gain altitude when splat! He hit my windshield on the driver's side, covering me with small pieces of glass. I drove all the way back home covered with small slivers of glass.

Since I only had liability coverage, I had to call my insurance company and find out where I could pay to have my windshield fixed. My agent gave me a number and I had to make an appointment on Saturday and meet them in a vacant parking lot. They changed it right there. Took about 45 minutes and cost me $212.12.

I guess the moral of the story is, don't count your chickens before they hatch.

5

THE BEAR STORY

There's a story my grandmother spoke about when my grandfather was taking a herd of cattle into Marathon.

This bear came upon the herd, and my grandfather couldn't shoot it, so he had to rope it and bring it up to the campfire. He couldn't just shoot it when it appeared near the herd, because he was afraid the gunshot would cause a stampede.

And this is the way the rest of the story goes. They killed the bear. One of the other guys on the cattle drive shot it. I don't know what the difference was. You can't shoot it up there, but you can shoot it at the campfire. But anyway, they shot the bear.

Then my grandfather took it to town, to Marathon, and told Hallie to take it to the taxidermist, and have it made into a bearskin rug. It would make a very nice rug.

So, Hallie did what Roy said and took it to the taxidermist.

I guess the taxidermist made a 911 emergency call to the game warden. He called the game warden and told him that my grandfather had killed this bear. Well, it wasn't long before the game warden looked up my grandfather and fined him $25 for killing the bear out of season and without a permit.

My grandfather was not a happy man. I guess back then $25 was a lot of money. You know, it's still a lot of money.

We had that bearskin rug for years and years. I don't know what happened to the rug, but the bear's head is in the Hallie Stillwell Hall of Fame Museum in a glass display case. So you can still see the head.

All that's left of Roy's bear

6

A SHUTTLE STORY

Back in the eighties, when we were really busy, I mean really, really busy during spring break, an unusual thing happened. My mother told me this story.

We had a lot of shuttles that year. Everyone in the family had to help with the shuttles.

What is a shuttle? It is when people pay us to help them with a float trip. They usually pick up a driver at Stillwell's and our driver takes them to their "put-in" spot on the river. Our driver waits while they unload their canoes and all their camping stuff, and then our driver brings their car back here to the store. Then in two or three days (or however long they plan to be on the river), we deliver their car to La Linda and it will be waiting for them when they come off the river.

Well that year we had about 30 cars parked across the road, ready and waiting to be dropped off at La Linda. When all the cars had been returned to their owners and everybody was off the river, my mother noticed that there was one truck left. She asked everyone if they knew who that truck belonged to. Had we possibly forgotten to deliver a shuttle?

But no one, it seems, had driven that truck as part of a shuttle. After my mother exhausted herself and was at her wits end trying to figure out how we came up with an extra car, she called the border patrol.

When the border patrol came, they also brought a drug dog. My mother was sitting on the porch and was watching the border patrol as they worked. They inspected the truck very closely and finally brought the dog out. The dog was very quiet. Never made a sound. The handler would walk around the truck and every time the dog would get to a wheel, he would sit down.

My mother said, "I guess there aren't any drugs."

The handler said, "That truck is full of drugs!"

"I didn't hear the dog bark," she replied.

He said, "They don't bark; they sit. So they don't alarm the drug runners. We have been looking for that truck and now we found it."

The drug folks had seen all those cars parked here and didn't know they were only here temporarily. I guess they were going to come back at some later time.

Bad guys never win.

7

A STORY MY SISTER LINDA TOLD ME

As the story goes, my sister Linda and her best friend Brenda were planning a trip to the ranch.

Brenda is a lover of animals. Every animal knew that they could show up on Brenda's doorstep and she would take them in.

Both Linda and Brenda were prone to be late. They were supposed to get up at 6:00 a.m. and get an early start. They talked it over and decided that they would leave even sooner, at 3:00 a.m. instead of 6 a.m.

I don't know for a fact what time they got off. I suspect they were late. Linda was driving. When they were almost to the ranch, Linda hit a rabbit. She made a remark that those rabbits were on a mission to commit suicide.

Well, it ruffled Brenda's feathers. She did not talk to Linda for three days. Even though it was an accident. Brenda cried for three days. Linda was beside herself. She tried to smooth things over. Brenda would have none of it.

Hallie noticed the tension between the two girls. I guess Linda had told her about hitting the rabbit.

The next time Brenda came in where Hallie was, Hallie said to her, "Do you run a fever with those fits?"

I guess that put it in perspective.

Brenda and Linda are still good friends to this day.

8

THE MEANEST COP IN DALLAS

One day my friend Marge and I went for a drive to get some Braun's ice cream. On the way back, I was driving along Garland Road, right in front of White Rock Lake in Dallas.

All of a sudden, I noticed a cop car behind us with his lights on. I pulled over to the side of the road. Of course, both of us hurried to fasten our seat belts.

The officer got out of his car and walked up to mine. I rolled down the window. I think he was the biggest, meanest cop in the Dallas/Fort Worth Metroplex.

In a very gruff voice, he asked to see my license and proof of insurance. I handed him my license and he went back to his car to run my handicapped license plate through the computer. It took about 20 minutes.

While he was gone, I looked for my proof of insurance. It just so happened that I had gotten a new card in the mail recently. I remembered telling myself that I would keep it in my desk so that I would know where it was. So when he came back and wanted my proof of insurance, I only had the expired one to show him. I told him about the new one, home in my desk.

He snatched my expired one and went back to his car. I know that he called my insurance agent to make sure I had insurance.

When he came back to the car, he handed me my expired insurance card and said, "Mrs. Patton, do you know what the speed limit is?"

I said, "No, sir."

"Do you know how fast you were going?"

"'Fraid not," I said.

He said, "You were going 45 in a 30!"

"Uh-oh!" I replied.

He scowled and said, "Mrs. Patton, are you any kin to the general?"

Now my grandmother always said to tell the truth and keep your credit good. I knew if I lied and said he was my great uncle or something like that he would know it was a lie. So, following her advice, I said, "Will it help?"

I have to say, he tried not to smile and keep that tough guy image, but I could see a little twinkle in his eye.

He said, "I'm not going to give you a ticket this time, but I don't want to see you driving through here like hell again!"

My reply was, "You sure as hell won't!"

9

LIFE INSURANCE

When Freddy was about 8 years old, I decided to get some life insurance.

I called an insurance company and they sent someone to the house. The man came in and asked a few questions. Then he proceeded to bring out his blood pressure cuff. He took my blood pressure and, of course, it was out of sight. He waited a few minutes and tried again, but it was still high. He then told me I would have to go to a doctor for a physical.

I went to the doctor they wanted me to go to. When the doctor came in, the first thing he did was take my blood pressure. Of course it was high. He then said he would turn the lights off and let me calm down a little and he would be back in a few minutes. He came back in about 30 minutes and it was still high.

He then went to phase two of the exam. Which was the breast exam. I was lying on the table and as he is mashing around on my left breast, he says, "Do you have any trouble with lumps, bumps or nodules?"

I said, "No, they are just painfully small."

He left the room quite suddenly. After a few minutes the nurse came in and asked what I said to the doctor. She said he was outside in the hall leaning on the wall. He was laughing so hard, he couldn't tell her what I said. I told her what had transpired and she left the room.

A short time later the doctor came back in the room and he took my blood pressure again. The doctor said it was still high.

My reply was, "If someone had just played with your tits, wouldn't your blood pressure be up?"

He bolted out the door and in a few minutes the nurse came back in and said, "What did you say now? He is on the floor in the hall and can't stop laughing."

I think they should have passed me and given me that life insurance, but they didn't.

I bet that doctor had never had such a good time at a patient's expense.

22

10

I WENT TO THE CHURCH FOR HELP

I had paid all my bills, sending checks to cover everything. I was expecting my child support to arrive. When I got it, it was not the $440 I was expecting, but only $135.

My ex, Fred, had taken it upon himself to send me the smaller amount, after deciding that $440 was too much. I asked my friend Claire what I should do. She said to go to the church.

I said, "I'm not active in the church."

She said, "It doesn't matter. The church will help you."

I went to the church and explained my situation. The Bishop listened while I explained the whole story.

The Bishop said he would pay two month's rent for me. The way it works is they don't give you cash. They write a check and then send it directly to the people involved.

The only thing Freddy and I had to do in exchange for the church's help was sweep the parking lot.

That is what I love about being LDS. They make you think it is not a handout…you do work for the money.

Nan with Freddy on May 10, 1970

11

I DIDN'T KNOW YOU HAD HEMORRHOIDS

When I was 19, I got very sick. I couldn't keep anything down.

I had been sick for about a week. My doctor put me in the hospital. My blood pressure was also out of control.

Once I got to the hospital, they kept me in a dark room. I wasn't allowed any visitors except my husband, and he couldn't stay very long.

After about three days the doctor came in and said, "I know what's wrong with you."

I asked, "Is it terminal?"

He said, "No, you're pregnant."

The first thing that went through my mind is, my mother is going to kill me.

They kept me in the hospital almost two weeks. I have never been that sick. I don't know if it was the hospital food or what.

They only served me two meals a day. Breakfast about 10:30 a.m. and lunch about 2:00 p.m. They served a snack about 9:00 p.m. For the snack, I got a banana every evening. I was trying to eat that banana so I could go home.

One night, the nurses came in and said they needed my room for a dying patient. They proceeded to try to get my bed, with me in it, through the door.

BAM, BAM, BAM! They finally realized that they would have to take off the rails in order to get the bed though the door. By that time it was too late. I lost the banana. It would not stay down.

The next day when my husband came in to see me, I said, "As soon as this baby is born, I'm going have a hysterectomy."

He looked at me and said, "I didn't know you had hemorrhoids."

At that very moment I knew my marriage was doomed.

12

THE DAY I QUIT SMOKING

Let me tell you this from the start: I was told from a very young age by my mother, if you smoke you will be "Written Out Of The Will."

After we were grown, I knew my sisters had all smoked at one time or another. It did not seem to bother them that they were going to be "Written Out Of The Will."

I started smoking after Freddy's father and I got a divorce. I will never forget that first cigarette I ever smoked. I got so sick and dizzy. Most people would have thrown them away and never looked back. Not me.

When Freddy got a little older, he would often ask me to quit smoking. I tried to quit. I even promised him I'd try to quit. The cigarettes always won. I was not one to promise God I'd quit. You don't want to break a promise to God.

On the day I was feeling like it would be a good day to quit smoking, I made a promise to Freddy that I'd quit. After a while I was craving a cigarette, so I went to my next-door neighbor and was sitting there smoking when Freddy came in.

He said, "You promised to quit smoking!" and ran out the door.

I went back to our apartment and Freddy was very upset with me.

I told him I was sorry. I never felt this bad before. I realized that I had broken one promise too many. I took him over to my mother's place to spend the night.

I got home from taking him to my mother's and I was really craving a cigarette by this time. I was looking in all the ashtrays to see if there was a butt I could smoke. I looked everywhere. I found none.

I was so desperate that in one weak moment, I said, "I promise you, God, I will never smoke a cigarette again as long as I live!"

The only thing I can say is, apparently God didn't want me to break my promise, so He took the desire away.

After I made the promise to God, I never wanted one. I have not had a cigarette in over 30 years and never even wanted one.

Nan and Freddy--
the picture that sat on the piano in the museum

13

A TRIP TO THE FIRE STATION

My sister Kay told me about one of her friends going to the fire station. She took her son to the fire station. She then started dating one of the firemen. Before long she ended up marrying one of the firemen.

So, I thought if it worked once, it will work twice. I thought I would give it a try.

The wheels started turning. I started vacation on Monday. I started asking Freddy if he wanted to go to the fire station. He was about seven years old. I thought any boy would like a visit to the fire station. He said no. I asked him again on Tuesday if he wanted to go to the fire station. He said NO again. It went on for the rest of the week.

Finally, Saturday I asked if he wanted to go to the fire station. After all, my week of vacation was almost over. He said, "I think you want to go the fire station more than I do."

So, off we went to the fire station. The station was in the next block. Freddy tried to act interested. I was so glad to see him asking questions. They took him on a tour. Even taking him in where they sleep and finally, they took him in the kitchen where they cook all their meals.

As luck would have it, they asked Freddy what he wanted to be when he was grown. He answered without hesitation: A POLICEMAN. I said to myself, "Fireman! Fireman!"

The fireman that was asking all the questions said, "I think your mother should take you to a police station."

14

THE DAY FREDDY THOUGHT HE WAS SUPERMAN

When Freddy was five years old, we moved into an apartment that had no screens on the windows. It was on the second floor. It had the windows that you had to crank the windows to open and close them.

One day I was walking through the house. I couldn't find Freddy anywhere. I called him and called him, but no answer.

All of a sudden I heard a faint, "Mama!"

I was surprised to see Freddy hanging by his little fingers on the ledge outside the window. I pulled him into safety.

Then I held him out the window, yelling, "Don't you know how far down that is!"

I've often thought about what might have happened if I hadn't gone to look for him. I am so lucky I did.

When Freddy was 42, I asked him what he remembered about that day. He said, "Don't you remember that I had my cape around my neck? I thought I was Superman!"

Freddy and Nan
about the time he thought he was Superman

15

A LESSON WELL LEARNED

My son Freddy started mowing yards when he was nine years old. He would often come in and say, "Mama, let's go out to eat!"

Since I was a single parent and struggling, I would sometimes reply, "Go mow a yard."

We would take the money he had just made and go out to eat. Over the course of his mowing years he bought us a washer, dryer and microwave. Not new, of course.

One of his customers was a man called Glenn D. Every other week Freddy would mow Glenn's whole yard, front and back. The next week he would only mow the front.

Glenn asked me if Freddy could help with some electrical work. He had hired a man to help him wire the back yard for lighting. I think he asked Freddy because he was young and could get in tight spaces. They worked all day. A few days later Glenn told me about the work, and also a story he overheard the man telling Freddy.

It went something like this:

His son had earned $40 mowing a yard. When his father asked him if he had given the money to his mother, the son replied that it was his money. He earned it and he was not going to give the money to his mother.

The next morning at breakfast when he got through eating, his mother said that will be $5. He had just had the breakfast special. He handed over his $5. After all, he made $40 and he wasn't worried about that little bit of money.

When he came in for lunch, you guessed it; his mother hit him up again for the $7.95 lunch special. When he came in for supper, he handed over all the money he had left to his mother.

Well, sometime later, when he was a senior in high school, he and a friend were going to go on a double date for the prom. His father asked him did he get any money from his mother. He said she had given him $20 and his father said, "Here's an extra $20 just in case."

When his friend found out his parents had given him $40, he was green with envy. He wanted to know if he didn't spend all of the money, what was he going to do with the money he had left.

The young man said, "Of course I will give back what I don't use."

His friend could not understand what he was trying to say.

He explained it this way. "If I need money, all I have to do is ask. My parents don't ask me what it is for. They just give it to me, no questions asked. I am so lucky that we have that bond of trust."

I think Freddy must have been listening that day. He mowed those yards and always handed over whatever he made. We had some pretty good meals.

16

SOMETIMES THE BAD GUY WINS

This is a true story. I bought my son Freddy an old 69 VW bug. It was called a semi-automatic. It had no clutch. The way it worked was, in order to shift, you depressed the brake half way in. I had never heard of such a thing, but Freddy wanted it and of course I bought it for him.

I wanted to get that car painted for his 17th birthday. I took it to Earl S. (I will not give the full name to protect the guilty.) Anyway Freddy and I took it in.

Freddy said, "Do you know how to drive a semi-automatic like this one?" They assured us that they did and even boasted that they had driven quite a few.

They called us a couple of days later and said the car was ready. I was to meet Freddy there.

I got there first and I noticed right away that they had painted the wheels the same color as the car. Since it was my first time having a car painted I looked around at all the other cars. Not a car on the lot had the wheels painted.

I went in the office and asked why they had painted the wheels. His reply was, "You do something nice for somebody and they complain!"

Freddy finally got there and I paid the guy and Freddy went to get his car. Thank goodness I hadn't left. Freddy came in and said his car wouldn't move. It wouldn't go forward or backward. I asked what they had done to the car.

The man I had just paid pulled out a paper saying they were not responsible for anything inside the car. We had a few words but to no avail.

I had to pay $65.00 to have the car towed and another $300.00 to get the car fixed. I talked to the man who fixed the car and he said it was forced into gear. He even gave me the part and showed how it had broken off by being forced. I asked him if he would write on the receipt his take on what happened.

I decided to take Earl S. to court. To do that, I had to pay $25.00 in court costs. I had to be in court at 8:00 a.m. I had to listen to all the other cases. All I wanted was the towing and the cost of the repairs. I didn't ask for money for my time away from work.

My case was the next to the last on that day. I knew something was up when they came back after lunch and the attorney for Earl S. came in arm in arm with the judge and they were talking about their golf game.

The judge ruled in favor of Earl S. The judge said the car was twenty years old and it was probably going to break anyway. I lost the fight. If you had asked me if I thought I was going to win, I would have told you, how could I not win?

Wonders never cease, do they?

17

THE DAY I WENT TO THE FORTUNE TELLER

We were married for seven years when my husband left me for a younger woman…and I was only 25!

My divorce attorney was going to meet me in Ft. Worth. My soon to be ex, Fred, was going to meet us there with his attorney.

It got off with a bad start. The minute my attorney started talking about child support for our five year old son, Fred said, "I'll go to jail before I pay child support!"

My attorney said, "Let's leave!"

So, off we went. Nothing was resolved. I felt discouraged.

I was driving down the street and all of a sudden I saw a sign for a fortune teller in a front yard. My car whipped around. I found myself in front of the fortune teller's door.

She dressed the part. She had on a dress and scarf. She asked me for $20. I had no paper money…just some change in the bottom of my purse. I found $7.00 all together.

She told me that a lock of my hair was buried between two dead people. She said I was under a curse.

The fortune teller made a list of things I was supposed to get at the grocery store: a dozen eggs, tea bags, one pound of coffee, and a loaf of bread.

I had heard of fortune tellers reading tea leaves, but tea bags???

She said all the groceries would be going to the church.

I was planning my getaway. Once I got in my car, I was never going to go that way again.

But she got in my car with me, and her grandchildren got in the car after her.

Her whole thing was that after I bought the groceries with my credit card, I was supposed to get cash back. They wouldn't let me have any cash back. It was 1975.

So she sent me in for more groceries: one gallon of milk, three pounds of coffee, two boxes of tea bags, and two loaves of bread.

Once we got back from the store, she took me inside. She said she wanted my phone number. I told her I didn't have a phone. That was the smartest thing I ever said!

She told me that I was to light a candle and then walk around my apartment. She also told me to put an egg in a shoe under the bed, and sleep on it.

I was never so glad to get out of there. I've never gone to a fortune teller since that awful day!

18

WHY I LOVE BUTTONS

When I was a little girl, I always enjoyed going over to Aunt Mabel's. Aunt Mabel was my grandmother's older sister.

We moved to San Antonio when I was 7 years old.

Every time I went back to Alpine to visit, I always went to Aunt Mabel's and she always made me chocolate chip cookies.

While she was making the cookies, she would bring her big button box out and ask me to string them. She would get a needle and a long thread. I would sit for it seemed like hours and string those buttons. After I would get through, I would go into the kitchen and tell her I was done.

She would bring them back into the living room and say, "I forgot. I need them separated by color."

So I would sit there and pull them all off the string and put them in piles by color. Then I would restring them, putting all the colors together.

I was born with cerebral palsy. I was three months premature. I only weighed 3 pounds and then lost weight so I was down to two and half pounds. Back in 1949 they didn't have the technology they have today. They didn't think I would make it through the first night.

As I reflect back on those happy times with Aunt Mabel, I realize that she was helping me with my eye-hand coordination.

That is why I love buttons. And that's why I love Aunt Mabel.

Nan at about age 7

19

RETIREMENT PARTY STORIES

Nan was affectionately referred to as a stand-up comic at Stillwell's. But her "career" started long before. The following stories were told at a phone company retirement party in 2001, and captured on video…

PEG

Everyone has heard this story, so I'll just say one word: Peg.

Right after I moved here from San Antonio, one day Charmaine came up to me and asked me if I'd like to go to lunch with her. And I thought, man, I'm really moving up. I'm not that San Antonio transplant any more. I've been accepted into the group.

So we decided to go across the street to a restaurant.

So you have to visualize this. We're in the middle of Commerce Street. I wear an AFO, which is a leg brace. And Charmaine says to me, while we're in the middle of the street, "Well, Nan, tell me. Where is your leg cut?"

I said, "My leg cut?"

She said, "You know, below the knee or above the knee?"

I said, "Charmaine, my leg's not cut. That is just a leg brace."

And she goes, "Oh, hee hee, hee. Someone told me you have an artificial leg."

I said, "No! I do not have an artificial leg."

So we went in and had lunch.

Of course, that set me back about 20 years. When I got home, I was still crying.   My son, Freddy, was there and I said, "Freddy, Charmaine thinks I have an artificial leg, and if she thinks I have an artificial leg, then everybody in the phone company thinks I have an artificial leg."

And Freddy said, "Mother, just consider the source and forget it. Don't worry about it!" and then he goes, "Come on, Peg, let's go eat!"

So ever since then, everybody started calling me "Peg."

A BLIND DATE

Well, right after I'd gone through the big D, you know, D-I-V-O-R-C-E, a friend of mine said, "Nan would you like to go on a blind date with my boyfriend and his best friend? There is just one little problem. He walks with a slight limp."

I said, "That's all right" as I had this vision of us both limping off into the sunset together. Because I had a little limp myself.

So that day I started getting ready about 6 a.m. By the time he got there, I was all studded out and ready to go.

When my date pulled up, Fred looked out and said, "Oh my gosh, Mom, oh, my gosh!"

So I went out and peeked through the window blinds. And my "slight limp" was a double amputee. And he didn't have state of the art limbs…they didn't bend.

We went to the opera, and we were up in the balcony. We had to stand the whole time because he couldn't sit.   For some reason, he fell in love with me and… that's far enough for that story.

RESTAURANT CODE WORDS

A guy went into a restaurant. The waitress came up and said, "Are you ready to order? What can I get you?"

The customer replied, "Yes, I am. I want a BLT/NT."

She said, "I know what a BLT is---bacon, lettuce, and tomato, but I don't know what NT means."

He rolled his eyes and said, rather rudely, "Not Toasted!"

"Oh, ok." So she placed the order. Soon she took it over to him and left to tend to another customer.

He took a bite. When she looked back, he was motioning to her to come back to his table.

She went back to him and said, "Is there a problem?"

He declared, "S-O-B!"

And she said, "What?"

He said, "Soggy On Bottom."

She replied, "S-H-I-T…Shoulda Had It Toasted!"

OVERSLEPT

I overslept. I used to call my friend Marge every morning and wake her up. I always used an alarm clock. But this time I called her and said "Marge! I overslept!"

"You overslept? Oh shit!"

So I rushed over there to pick her up… and she goes, "We've got to go down and pay my cable bill."

"We've got to pay the cable bill? Can't it wait until after work??"

"No!" she declared. So we go and pay the cable bill, which means I'm driving to work a different way than I am used to.

So from this new way, I'm trying to get on the HOV lane. And I'm thinking…I've only got a quarter of a mile to move over four lanes.

So, I'm driving, looking back over my left shoulder, looking how and when to get in. Now, I'm ADD. So, I'm looking back, I'm looking back. And all the traffic is whizzing by me on the left. Nobody lets me in. Now, the guy behind me wanted the HOV lane, but he didn't wait for me to get over there, he had to cut me off.

So I'm looking back, still looking back, and Marge is going, "Oh, oh, Nan, Nan!"

And I'm saying, "Not now, Marge! Not now!" and I'm looking back, looking back when I finally turned around forward and BOOM!

I hit that cement barricade wall going 50 miles an hour!   So I'm still sitting there, right up on the wall, gripping the wheel. And Marge is going, "Oh..., oh…., oh!"

And I said, "NOT NOW!"

People are driving by giving me the Texas Howdy (the finger), because I'm backing up traffic. Like I woke up that day and said, "I want to total my car today."

I'm sitting there. Finally someone called 911.

Soon somebody tapped on my window. "Are you ok, are you breathing?"

He taps on my window again, and says, "Are you hurt?"

I shook my head no.

"Do you know where you are?" I nodded yes.

"Do you know who you are?" I nodded yes.

"Will you tell me?" I shook my head no.

Then I said, "Ok, I'll give you my first name. You have to guess the rest of it." I drew my finger across my forehead, "STUPID--right here on my forehead: STUPID!"

They carted Marge off in an ambulance, and I'm still sitting there. Everybody is gone. I'm still sitting in the car and everybody is giving me the Texas Howdy again.

And finally, a guy says, "Do you need a ride home? Do you need a ride somewhere?"

And I said, "Yeah, I don't feel like going to work."

He led me over to the police car and he opened the back door, and I said, "Are you arresting me?"

"No Ma'am," So I got in.

Have any of you ever been in a police car? There are no doorknobs in there; there are no locks. I mean, once you are in there, you are IN there. And they've got those wire gate things.

So I got in and he said I was the first one to ride in that back seat. So I'm going, how come I'm not thrilled?

I guess it was on TV…the traffic helicopter caught it on camera. And they were saying while watching us, "Should I get on the HOV lane, should I not get on the HOV lane?"

We made the TV and radio.

JACK-IN-THE-BOX ADVENTURE

Marge thought being my friend was going to be easy. We'd been friends for a long time.

One night we were in my old car…it was a mini-van. The window was broken on my side. It wouldn't roll down. We were going to the Jack in the Box drive through.

My window wouldn't roll down, so I drove in the wrong way. So Marge rolled down her window, and you should have seen the look on that guy's face!

She said, "We'd like four tacos, and can you make it quick?"

But it was funny…no other cars came around. So I just drove on through, no problem.

20

THE DAY KAY SAVED MY LIFE

Before I tell you about the day Kay saved my life, I have to give you a little history. This is what happened and all are true events. Hold on to your hat.

My friends Barbie, Aida, and I had lap-band surgery for weight loss in 2003. Needless to say, before the surgeries, we were each quite pudgy.

Back in those days we didn't know what we were getting into. We went to the doctor together and even went in to consult with him at the same time.

He asked us a few questions and said it was up to the insurance company to ok the surgery. He sent us over across the street for blood work and that was it. We waited for a couple of weeks and we were all approved.

That was the beginning of my journey.

Since Barbie was so small, the doctor said it would take her longer to lose the weight. Aida weighed 20 pounds more than I did. So I was expecting her to lose the weight faster than any of us.

After the surgery, we could only have clear liquids for about two weeks. I remember that when we could finally have something else, Barbie and I went to El Chico for tortilla soup and it was the best soup in the world. It tasted so good. We thought we had died and gone to heaven.

On our second office visit after the surgery, we each had to get fluid put in our band. The lap band surgery always leaves a "port" just under your skin, near your stomach, so they can make any adjustments to the lap band. They inject a saline solution in the port and it expands the balloon around the band, thus restricting the amount of food you can eat.

Everything was going fine until they got to me. After sticking me multiple times, prodding around for my port, the doctor told me my port was put in upside down. He wanted me to go to another doctor and have surgery on the port to put it in the correct position. He made all the arrangements for me.

Soon it was the day for surgery. I reported at 6:00 a.m. as I was told. Keep in mind I had never met this doctor.

I was in the hall, waiting to go into the operating room. I thought to myself, I hope I get to at least meet the doctor before I go under the knife. I was glad when he came over and introduced himself. Before I went into surgery he came back over and asked me if I knew how much fluid to put in my band.

I said, "Have you ever done this before?" and he said he had.

After that surgery, I thought it all had been corrected. It wasn't until sometime later I found out that the port was still upside down.

I went back to my first doctor and I mentioned that I felt I was losing weight too fast. I had lost over 50 pounds in only three months. He said, "I bet you haven't been less than 200 pounds in years. Do you want to be on a cane for the rest of your life?"

As we were leaving, I turned to Barbie and said, "I can't believe I just paid a $20.00 co-pay to get my ass chewed out!"

In the meantime, I retired in early 2004 and moved out to the ranch. I was having my house built there and so I was living in my travel trailer. There were no mirrors except for one over the sink. I did not know how bad I looked.

My sister Kay and her husband, David, came out to help during Spring Break in March. I was so weak by then that I couldn't hold my head up. I was planning to go to Dallas to see my doctor but I was too weak to drive the 10 hours it took to get there. Kay offered to take me to San Antonio and put me on a plane to Dallas. I took her up on the offer.

She decided to leave on Saturday, cutting her Spring Break by one day. When we got home to San Antonio, it was 8:00 p.m. and we were exhausted. She asked me where I wanted to sleep. I said I had acid reflux so bad I would have to sleep sitting up on the couch. She fixed me a bed on the couch and went to go brush her teeth.

Then she came rushing back and said, "I think we should take you to the hospital right now."

I said, "What's the problem? Did you see me dead on the couch?"

She had a shocked look on her face and asked, "How did you know?"

I had just had the same vision myself.

So we went to the hospital right away. Kay dropped me off at the emergency room while she parked the car. I went in and spoke to the man behind the bullet proof glass. He wanted to know what my problem was.

I tried to explain about the lap band and told him that I hadn't been able to eat for a couple of weeks. He was very impatient and said, "Cut to the chase!"

They put you in priority status. I guess mine was not life threatening. I saw him put my chart on the very bottom of the stack.

Kay came in after parking the car, and sat down beside me. I guess she was trying to keep my mind off of things. She would say, "See that woman over there? She thinks she's had a heart attack. It's nothing more than she's having a gall bladder attack."

The nurse came in and asked the woman what she had to eat. Fajitas, sour cream, guacamole and flour tortillas. They came in sometime later and said she did not have a heart attack. Instead it was a gall bladder attack.

As the night wore on, my sister continued to amaze me with her insight. Another girl came in and she thought her foot was broken. Kay said it was a bad sprain. They wheeled her off and a short time later, after having her foot x-rayed, it did prove to be a bad sprain.

We sat there until 4:00 a.m. Sunday morning when they finally sent me to x-ray. The x-ray showed that my lap band had slipped. My stomach was in the shape of an hour glass. The top of the stomach had fallen over the band, blocking everything. I was starving to death. No food would go in.

They finally put me in a room about 6 a.m. My electrolytes were all messed up. I had to wait a day before they could do surgery to correct the problem.

The day of surgery, the doctor came in about 7:30 a.m. He said, "I will try to do it laproscopically," which would be a relatively minor surgery. Of course, with my luck, it turned into a major surgery. When I woke up, I had about 14 staples going down and across my stomach. I was in the hospital about a week.

Kay took me back to her house in San Antonio. She gave me a pint of chocolate milk. I forgot to tell her I was lactose intolerant. All I wanted to do was to go to bed and feel sorry for myself.

It wasn't long after I drank that milk that I had to get up and go the bathroom. I spent half the night running to the bathroom. After about the fifth time, it didn't hurt so bad when I rolled out of bed.

Kay has saved my life on more than one occasion. If she hadn't insisted that I go with her to San Antonio, I would not be writing this chapter.

Nan and Kay at Stillwell's, New Year's Eve, 2011
Kay was staying there to care for Nan,
then in the later stages of the disease
that would take her life the following July.

Showing Nan Michigan's Leelenau Peninsula
From left: Ed & Mary Rothgarber, Uhl & Nancy Donovan, Mary
Meyer, Nan, Eldon & Ann Whitford

Enjoying the sights in Minnesota

21

TRAVELS UP NORTH

These are posts from the Stillwell Store website, written by Nan after she returned from her visits to Michigan and Minnesota in the summer of 2010.

In Michigan, I had a great time with the Whitfords. At a party in my honor, various folks from Michigan and elsewhere showed up for a visit. From the Reed City/Hersey, Michigan area were Larry and Suzi Neiderhyde, Phil and Wendy Noder, Chuck and Barb Schneider, and Terry and Jan Teesdale, all of whom have stayed at the Stillwell's Ranch and RV Park. Other Stillwell regulars who came to the party were Ed and Mary Lou Rothgarber from Suttons Bay, Bonny Everett and Dutch Zonderman also from Suttons Bay, Carol and Glen Dunn from Lansing, Josh and Abby Whitford and Heather Imhoff from Wyoming, MI, and Mary Meyer from Indiana. Uhl and Nancy Donovan from South Dakota surprised everyone when they drove in during the party.

I stayed at the Whitfords for several days. They took me around Michigan quite a bit. I got to see Lake Michigan, Sleeping Bear Dunes, the Traverse City/Suttons Bay areas, and the Leelenau Peninsula, all thanks to Ed and Mary Lou, who live in Suttons Bay.

Eldon and Ann took me to the "flat-land" farming area of central Michigan, where I met Eldon's parents, Gene & Dorothy Whitford, and Ann's mom, Mary Sievert. I also got to the Grand Rapids area, where I flew in, and visited Josh and Heather. I also met the Reed City McDonald's morning coffee group…who filled me in on a lot of local gossip and tall tales, including the Dogman of Luther. I met Abby's mom, Elyse Ermatinger, too.

Michigan is beautiful, green, and wet! The green and wet part doesn't happen often at Stillwells!!

After Michigan, I continued on to Minnesota for a long weekend near Duluth, including the barn-warming party hosted by Dene and Sally Halvorson, long-time Stillwell campers.

I flew out of the little town of Muskegon, MI, on the coast of Lake Michigan. When I landed in Duluth, Minnesota, there to greet me were Dene and Sally Halvorson, my official hosts for the long weekend, as well as other Minnesota friends, Bob and Gayle Herr. Bob and Gayle have become Stillwell regulars along with Dene and Sally.

I spent all my time with the four of them as they entertained me in the wilds of northern Minnesota. Dene and Sally have a lovely home out in the woods about 45 minutes from Lake Superior. We enjoyed several meals on their screened-in porch. The food and the company were great!

What a gorgeous area they live in! One day we went out on a pontoon boat owned by their friends, Steve and Linda Hadley. We had a lovely time out on the lake behind the Hadley's home. We were joined that day by Dan Lewis and Kim Hambrick, and Kim's daughter, Nicole.

Another day we took a boat ride out on Lake Superior. It was a real treat to be surrounded by so much water! They told me you can take a glass and drink right out of Lake Superior, it's so pure. I didn't test that theory, though, and I don't know if I ever will! But it sure is beautiful!

Dene and Sally had a party on Saturday night to celebrate the completion of their new barn. The party included lots of great food, good people, good music, and dancing. Dene and Sally taught everyone how to do the Texas Two-Step.

I enjoyed a few days with Sally's parents, Charlotte and Bob Barina. I worked with Charlotte splitting the homemade hot dog buns for the party. I met Dene's mother, Dorothy Halvorson. Marty, Dene and Sally's son, was also there, home for a visit after finishing college last spring. He's headed for grad school this fall.

One special guest at the party was Princess Pearl-E-Gates. (The Princess's real name is Patti Anderson.) She was dressed in a hula skirt and carried her magic wand (which on Earth would be known as a sprinkler wand). As part of the festivities, many of us paid for the privilege of dancing with the Princess, with our donations going to a fund to create a Memory Garden at the church.

Patty's husband, Dean, was at the party, too. He was gracious enough to help with the hay ride by driving one of the wagons for us to ride on. The kids really enjoyed the hay ride...and the adults did too!

I met so many wonderful people while I was in Minnesota, I can't remember all their names!

I headed back for Texas with new understanding of the places my Midwest/Northern friends call home when they are not here at Stillwell's.

Enjoying Minnesota's beauty

**With the Halvorsons in Minnesota, Sally (above) and
Dene (below)**

22

RADIOACTIVE NAN

Told on March 25, 2010, at the Hallie Stillwell Hall of Fame. Thanks to Barb Fisher for transcribing it from the video she made that night.

Well, I thought I had a stroke a few months ago. I didn't think anybody noticed anything was different, but one day Larry said I was slurring my words. I called my sister Kay, and she said I had to get to a doctor.

So I went to San Antonio to have all the tests. I went to the emergency room, because my sister told me to go straight to the emergency room. She had talked to her doctor about it, so I did.

If you ever need to go to the emergency room, go to the Texsan Heart Hospital in San Antonio. I was the only one there, and I'm standing up there, and the guy behind the bulletproof glass said, "Ma'am, what's your emergency?"

I said, "I've had a stroke."

So, he yelled "STROKE!" and this nurse came bolting out of the door.

She said, "Come with me quick! When did you have your stroke?"

I said, "Probably about two months ago."

"Oh." She had a startled look on her face.

Before I knew what happened, I was hooked up to IV's and everything. Well, they didn't keep me that long, which was amazing, just long enough to make me black and blue on both arms. After about three hours, they sent me home.

So next we went to my sister's heart doctor. (That's my older sister, Kay. Some of you may have met her. She's the boss. You do whatever she says.) Of course, Kay thinks I'm 12 and she has to go with me to every place I go.

Kay's doctor said, "Why are you here?"

And Kay said, "She's had a stroke."

Her doctor said, "I'm a heart doctor. I don't know anything about strokes."

And Kay said, "Oh."

Photo captured from the Fisher's video of Nan's telling of "Radioactive Nan"

So her doctor said, "Well, we'll set you up with a neurologist."

They set up the appointment. I went to this neurologist in two days. I went into the office---with Kay, of course.

I was sitting there in the office and the neurologist said, "Why are you here?"

And my sister said, "She's had a stroke."

He looked at me and he said, "Why do you think you've had a stroke?"

I said, "Well, my tongue feels like it's this big," showing with my hands a circle about the size of a basketball, "and I'm slurring my words."

He said, "Say 'Methodist'."

I said, "Methodist."

He said, "Say 'Episcopal'."

I said, "Episcopal."

He said, "You haven't had a stroke!"

I said, "Did you graduate from seminary, or medical school?"

So, the bottom line was, I didn't have a stroke. So, I had to tell people, if it sounds like I'm drunk, it's something else. It's not a stroke.

So they were still trying to figure out what was going on with me and decided to give me another test. I had to take this radioactive chemical stress test.

Well, I should have known there was something up when they came in with a lead container. It was at the end of a long pole, and everyone was standing way back. And so I'm sitting there with this lead container and this pole all by myself.

You know, the test is not that bad, but you have about three minutes of wholly not feeling good.

I was sitting there and the nurse - sitting way back there – said, "Are you all right?"

And I said, "I'm all right," and then right after that, "No, I don't feel good right now. You'd better bring me a bucket."

Well, have you ever seen them bring a fishing pole with a bucket on the end? Way over there? The feeling only lasted for a few seconds and then I felt all right.

After the chemical stress test was over, they gave me this piece of paper and they said, "Anytime you have to go through Border Patrol, you have to show them this piece of paper."

OK. So, we were on our way home to the ranch. Larry's driving. I was on the passenger side. We got to the outskirts of Del Rio. We went through the Border Patrol. I had all these papers ready. I was ready to tell them, you know, I've had this test. Larry rolled down the window.

They said, "Are you a US citizen?"

And Larry said, "Yes."

They didn't ask me. We just went on, and I thought, I don't know what the big deal is. Then when we come south out of Marathon, we don't have to stop at the Border Patrol station heading home towards the ranch.

So, the next day Ann Whitford and I had to go to Marathon to do a shuttle. Ann was driving the shuttle car, and I was driving my Ranger pickup. When I'm doing a shuttle run, I always want to be the lead car, in case a deer jumps out. I'd rather it hit my car than the shuttle car that's not mine.

So, Ann was behind me, driving the shuttle car, as we pulled up to the Border Patrol station. My driver's side window on my truck was broken and wouldn't roll down, so I had to open the door.

There was this twelve year old standing there in his uniform, and he asked me if I'm a US citizen. I opened the door to answer him, saying, "My window won't roll down."

Toot toot toot! When I opened my door, every alarm in the whole place went off!

He stepped back and said, "Ma'am, have you had a medical test?"

And I said, "As a matter of fact, I have."

Other Border Patrol people came over by my pickup, and I was thinking to myself, that I left my medical paperwork in Larry's car.

So, they said, "Ma'am, do you mind pulling over?"

And I said, "No problem." I pulled over to the side.

Ann drove up behind me, went around, and parked her shuttle car to wait for me. She got through with no problem, of course, but she saw that they had stopped me.

Then Border Patrol said, "Step away from the car."

I got out of the car. Fifteen people were going in my car, under my car, behind my car, looking at everything. They have a little bench there outside the patrol station, so we sat down.

So, we were sitting out there and it was cold. It was early morning and I was getting chilled. I was sitting there, and this little guy - he kept coming over - at a distance, and he said, "Ma'am, you don't look like a terrorist!"

I said, "I'm not a terrorist."

"Ma'am, do you have the paperwork for your medical test?"

"No, but I can tell you where it is!"

"Well, hold on a minute, Ma'am," and he went over to consult with his boss.

I was just wearing a light vest and I was getting more and more chilled.

So when he came back, I said, "Do you mind if I go to my car? I'm a little chilled and I need to get out of this cold air."

He walked with me - a couple of paces back, of course-- to my truck and he kept saying, "Ma'am, you don't look like a terrorist."

As I was walking to my pickup, he said, "Please, don't run."

I'm thinking to myself, as I am walking with my usual limp, look at me! You think I'm going to run?

So, I got in my pick-up and I said, "Sir, do you mind if I start the engine and heater, because it's cold out here?"

He said, "No problem. But please don't drive off."

"I'm not going to drive off," I replied, but the moment I started that car, I was surrounded again by Border Patrol people.

"Ma'am, step away from the car!"

So I had to get out of the car again, and they escorted me, at a distance, to the inside of the Border Patrol station.

Have you ever been inside a Border Patrol station? I think they've got cells in there. It's very plain, bare walls. They only have one bathroom. Everyone has to use the same bathroom.

So then I had to wait. They had to send to Alpine for a special Border Patrol Guru. He would bring this Geiger counter thing to tell exactly what was in my body and what medical test I had. It took an hour and a half for him to arrive. All the time, I was sitting there, while Ann waited outside for me.

This man finally came in. He spoke with such a heavy German accent, I could hardly understand a word he said. Then he asked me if I'm a US citizen!

He got out this Geiger counter thing and he went over my body with a wand. Toot toot toot toot.! Why he had to go behind me I don't know, but he went toot toot toot! behind me and up my back. Then he walked away. He finally came back and he said he was done with all the tests.

We still had to call the doctor and have him fax the papers - the order for the tests I had.

An hour and a half later we finally got to go. As we were leaving, they handed me this piece of paper and said, "Anytime you come through here (you're radioactive for 30 days - depending on how well your kidneys are working), bring this paper and we'll only hold you a maximum of 30 minutes or so."

I told them, "I just won't come back until I'm not radioactive anymore."

Then Ann, in her infinite wisdom, said, "Aren't you going to San Antonio tomorrow?"

I went, "Oh, darn!" So, they told me to call in the morning before I left the ranch and let them know I was coming.

So, the next morning we were packing up, getting ready to go. I called them. I said, "We're coming through. I want to make this as painless as possible. I don't want to spend an hour and a half on the side of the road."

"Oh, no problem, Ma'am. What vehicle are you driving?"

"F150 pick-up, champagne color, and we're pulling a trailer full of crushed - Coke and beer cans."

So, on our way north to Marathon, we drove up to the Border Patrol station. They didn't even slow us down. They waved us on through, as though I was not radioactive anymore.

So, the moral of this story is: If you're going to be a terrorist, be the passenger, not the driver.

And every word of this is true - maybe a little exaggeration. Most of it is the absolute truth.

Part II

Stories about Nan

Nan and Kay with W.T.

23

SIS

by Kay Pizzini

by Kay Pizzini

Written in August of 2013, just two months before Kay herself passed away unexpectedly…

My first memory of Nan was when they brought her home from the hospital. The first thing that came out of my mouth was "Who ironed her?"

She was born three months premature and stayed in the hospital for three months. They kept her lying on her one side to keep her heart from being crushed.

My mother did not know she was pregnant with Nan until she went into labor due to the fact that she was still nursing my sister Linda, moving from the Martin Ranch to Alpine, and starting graduate school at Sul Ross University.

Around the sixth month of Nan's life, my mother knew something was wrong with her because she could not sit up in the highchair. She kept sliding down. Nan was diagnosed with CP (cerebral palsy).

I remember my mother saying Nannette had to learn to crawl, so I would work her arms and my mother would work her legs.

By her nature Nan always had to do everything we (myself & Linda) did. It just took her longer. Before she passed, I asked her if she ever learned to ride a bike. She wrote on her board: "16 years old". She didn't give up on anything.

The other amazing thing she did, was teaching herself to crochet by sitting across from me. She watched me crochet and then she crocheted everything backwards. She crocheted much better than I ever did.

I miss her spirit in my life.

24

I NEED YOUR BACK

by Marilyn Shackelford

The Shackelfords are West Texas natives, living in Marathon, as well as on a beautiful ranch south of Stillwell's, overlooking Mexico.

We have known Nan all our lives.

When she was born, it was thought that she had polio, and the people all rallied around to help. As we all know now, that was not the case, but the cerebral palsy was taking its toll on her.

As time went on, Nan became a very independent, self-sufficient person. She raised a wonderful son, Freddy, and retired from South Western Bell Telephone Company.

That was just the beginning of her life. She moved to Stillwell ranch and began running the RV Park and Store.

This was what her life was all about. She had dreamed of moving back to her roots.

Nan had grown into a comic and a storyteller. One day, on our way to the ranch, we stopped at the store, which we often did, and Nan said, "Marilyn, come in and sit down. I need to talk to you."

My first thought was, "Oh crap, what have I done now?"

She came in and sat down, and began to tell me that she was the only real Stillwell that was at the ranch. She said, "I love to talk and tell stories."

"Oh yeah, I know that," I replied.

"Well, I need your back if I tell a story that is not exactly right. In other words, don't correct me in front of anyone."

That was our pact and I'm sticking to it.

Nan loved to watch Macky and me dance. She would call to make sure we were going to the dance at the Post or coming to the ranch when they had bands playing. She also loved to dance with Macky.

What a jewel we lost! Just when her life was beginning.

Macky and Marilyn Shackelford

My bet is she is still telling stories in Heaven and she is checking to see if I am holding up my end of the deal.

Macky and my biggest regret is that Nan never got to go to our side of our ranch to see our house. That was a big plan for her, but the situation was not to be.

Rest in Peace, Nan.

Patsy Cavness with the Crafty Ladies Group from Marathon

**Back row from left: Sande Pedro, Hildy Santos, Anne Carter, Jackie Boyd, Mary Mitchell, Marian Collins, Connie Springfield
Front row from left: Isobel Shackelford, Jodie Freeman, Patsy Cavness, Susan Spears, LaVerne Avery**

25

A LIFELONG FRIEND

by Patsy Cavness

I first met Nan as a small child. My grandparents lived next door to her grandparents, the Stillwells.

I stayed with Grandmother a lot so when Dadie, Nan's mother, and the girls came next door, we would go over to visit. One day Nan reached in the goldfish bowl and pulled out a goldfish and put it in her mouth.

Dadie and the girls moved to San Antonio, so I didn't see them much over the years.

When Nan retired and moved to Stillwell Store, I got to know her again and she wanted to join our quilt club. We met on Thursdays from 1-4 p.m. She came when she could get away from the store. She would come rushing in and started telling stories and we were all laughing. Then she would sit down at the quilt we were working on and say, "Now I have to quilt some stitches so I can say I helped make this quilt!"

We made two quilts a year. We sold chances on each one. One was for our own quilt show and the other one was for a fundraiser for the Health Clinic. We made about $800 to $1000 on each one.

Nan got sick and her voice was not good. She went to several doctors before she found out she had a terrible disease. She got worse as time went by and couldn't come to our meetings. Several of us went down to Stillwells to visit her. She was much worse so Rosalinda went down and spent the day with her. Nan couldn't talk so she wrote on a whiteboard to tell us what she wanted.

One day Connie and I spent the day with her while Kay went to Alpine to tend to business. I stayed in her bedroom in the back of the store with her, and Connie answered the phone and waited on customers in the front. Nan always had on her make-up and earrings and necklace and all and a beautiful smile and her thumbs up, which meant "Ok, great!"

Rosalinda and I spent the afternoon in the hospital with her and Kay the day before she passed.

What a great and wonderful person I had for a friend! I will always remember her.

Nan's son came on Labor Day, 2013 and put a beautiful stone at her grave.

26

REDISCOVERING DANCING AND SOME IMPORTANT LIFE LESSONS
--THANKS TO NAN

by David Moffitt

Nan had a significant influence on my life, particularly after I retired in 2004. I've always had an affection for the Big Bend area, dating back to my first visit as a child back in 1958, and continuing to many visits as an adult beginning in 1972.

In October 1992, I made a special return visit to the Big Bend to attend the annual meeting of the Big Bend Natural History Association (then led by Rick Labello), where I was introduced to a very distinguished looking elderly lady-- none other than Hallie Stillwell. I had no idea who she was, but once I read a copy of her first book, "I'll Gather My Geese", I began to get some insight about the people who first settled the beautiful part of Texas that kept drawing me back, and the Stillwell family meant a great deal to me.

During the 1990's and early 2000's other obligations kept me away from the Big Bend. However, after I retired in 2004, I began returning to this magical place.

I believe my first meeting with Nan was probably in 2006. At the time I did not own an RV, but after spending a few hours at the Stillwell Store, I began to think of it as a great place to "hang out" while enjoying the Big Bend. Nan had that special effect on you-- she became your best friend almost instantaneously!

So in February 2007, after attending my first Pioneer Reunion, I bought a travel trailer and headed to Stillwell's. Although my initial stays were not always the longest, I was quickly able to claim the title of a Stillwell "frequent flyer," having shown up at least six times in 2008 alone.

Nan always seemed so excited to see me (or anyone else), which probably explains why I felt so comfortable coming back--and back, and back!

David and Nan share a dance at the Trailride BBQ

In 2009, I happened to be there during the Trail Ride. I remember returning one evening after hiking the South Rim Trail in the park for my first time (about 12-13 miles) only to find Nan egging me on to participate in the dance they were having that night after the barbecue.

That's when I rediscovered dancing-- something I had not done for years. So, not only had Nan "nudged" me into RV travel, she had gotten me out on the dance floor. Nan was so manipulative!

As good friends as Nan and I became, we definitely were not on the same page, politically speaking. She used to forward emails to me from people who were far more conservative in their political leanings than I was. After receiving several of these (not welcomed to me) messages from Nan, I tried to come up with a "diplomatic" way to respond to her, without jeopardizing our friendship.

So, I asked her, "If I told you I totally disagree with everything the person in the forwarded email had to say, would you still dance with me?"

Being perhaps more diplomatic than I, Nan quickly responded, "Of course I will dance with you!"

And, that was the last "political" discussion Nan and I ever had.

Nan was often frustrated because the plans she had for the store and campground ran counter to what W. T., her stepfather, had in mind. One evening I was visiting at the store when both Nan and Kay were there for Spring Break. Rather innocently, Nan asked Kay who was "in charge," as one of them was going to close at 9:00 PM. Just as the question was posed, W. T. appeared from the back of the store and stated rather emphatically, "I'm in charge!" I felt sorry for both of them, as it seemed that as long as W. T. was around, there was going to be no question as to who was "in-charge!"

When Nan first started having problems with her speech, she once emailed me that she was trying to find out what was wrong with her voice. I rather "flippantly" responded that I never knew Nan to be at a loss for words. Little did I know that Nan was in the early stages of the disease that would ultimately claim her life!

Some months later I was there for a visit, and both her friend Barbie and another one of Nan's former Southwestern Bell co-workers were there. When I was introduced to Janie, Nan quickly wrote on her dry-erase board, "Another SW Bell 'ding-a-ling!'"

I never met someone who could face such a horrible prognosis with such bravery and a sense of humor. What a great lesson Nan was teaching all of us!

In July 2012, I took a long trip to the Pacific Northwest. On my way back I stopped in Van Horn, TX at lunchtime and called the Stillwell Store. Kay answered and told me that Nan had died Thursday evening, and that her funeral would be on Monday.

I drove down on Sunday afternoon, and attended her funeral in Marathon (just as I had done with W. T. the previous fall). Sometimes, I think Nan timed her death so I could be there for her funeral. Other times I think I could have never been that lucky.

All I really know is that I have been incredibly fortunate to have known Nan and all her friends!

After losing her voice completely and having to use a feeding tube, Nan wrote me on her dry-erase board, "I think God is punishing me. He took away my two favorite activities-- talking and eating!"

What an incredible lady she was!   All our lives have been so enriched by her kindness!

27

"HALLIE ALWAYS LIKED ME BEST"
Our Introduction to Nan

by Richard and Barbara Fisher

Richard and Barbara are adept at both still and video photography, and have created many photos and videos about the Stillwell experience and Big Bend. From "Radioactive Nan" to various music programs at the museum, as well as "On the Porch", for years they recorded the people and activities that made Nan and Stillwell's special to so many people.

Dick and I have different remembrances of the details of how we first met Nan. What a surprise! I will try to reconcile the stories for you.

In February of 1997, a month and a half after retiring from our jobs, we took off to visit Big Bend National Park, and other parts of the Southwest which we had never visited before. We spent 10 days in the park before heading further west.

We continued this winter sojourn for a number of years, and each year we added a hike or drive in Big Bend which we had not previously done. After perhaps five years we decided to visit Black Gap Wildlife Management Area to see what it was about.

We stopped at the Stillwell Store to buy some ice cream, as I recall. I do not remember who we might have met in the store on that occasion, but there was a group of people standing around, staring at us, as though they were thinking, "Where did these dudes come from and where did they get those funny hats?" Can't have been Nan. She would have started a conversation.

Something about the experience aroused our interest and when we saw Hallie's book, "I'll Gather My Geese", at the park store, I suggested we buy it. Dick decided that it would be more appropriate to buy it at Stillwell's, so that is what we decided to do.

We returned to the Stillwell Store on another day, purchased the book, and had a long conversation with Hallie's granddaughter, Linda, Nan's sister, who was behind the counter that day. She stamped the book with Hallie's signature stamp, and we asked her if she would sign it also. She agreed to do so, and said that her sister, Nan, was in the front room of the store and would sign the book, too.

We walked into the front room where Nan was sewing - I think a quilt - with a friend. We talked a few minutes and she signed Hallie's book with her name and added "Hallie always liked me best," but added in a hushed voice, "Don't tell Linda." So, that was our introduction to Nan and her marvelous sense of humor.

The following year we visited the ranch with our trailer for one night on our way into the park for our usual visit. Each year after that we did the same, eventually adding a day or two at the ranch to listen to the stories and eventually discovering the evening music program with the Whitfords. Eventually we were staying the entire 10 days at the ranch before heading farther west.

We also added a stop at the ranch on our way east and found that was a good time for seeing the prickly pear cacti blooming. It was always great to visit with Nan and listen to her stories about her family and the ranch and the Big Bend area and to enjoy the social atmosphere and the unique personalities of everyone who lived there, or "snow-birded" there.

I recently visited a travel website that had ratings on campgrounds, one of which was Stillwell's. There were a half a dozen four star ratings, followed by a one star rating. The comment under the one star rating was that this person could not understand where all these four star ratings were coming from. Had to be a one nighter, who never participated in the activities. Probably stayed inside and was frustrated that he couldn't watch football. Some folks just don't get it. His loss.

**Barbara, camera in hand, and Richard Fisher,
sitting with Joan Payne at a Stillwell campfire.**

**Cindy Bolton and her mother, Doris Downard,
with Nan at the Stillwell Store**

28

THE DAY I MET NAN

by Cindy Bolton

I never will forget the date of when I met Nan. It was the day after my 50th birthday, which was September 22, 2006, so we met on September 23.

I had heard and read of Hallie, the "ranching woman" or that is how I had remembered it. My family was with me to celebrate my birthday and one thing I wanted to do was visit the Hallie Stillwell Hall of Fame Museum. So here we took off from the Big Bend Park.

As we drove up, as I later told Nan, I seriously thought the place had dried up and blown away. Then we came to the store. Even though we didn't pick straws as to who would go in, I spoke up to go in, to be the strong one, and take one for the family.

As I walked in, in a way it was like another time and place…and then a sweet voice spoke from the back saying, "I'll be there in a minute."

I didn't know who or what would come out, but, as I said, I was taking one for the family! Here came the one I would come to know and love as part of the family, Nan, with a big smile and those big eyes of hers.

She was exclaiming, "Oh, let me get my camera and take a picture of you! I haven't seen anyone for days!"

And for a moment I was believing it! I just started laughing. The rest, as I told Nan, is history. My stepfather, Robert, who was very ill at the time, and my mother, Doris, and I visited the museum and then came back to the porch to rest and visit Nan.

It was the most wonderful time of my life, and life-changing forever. Nan told stories of the area, and we visited with locals as they stopped on the porch for a while.

My stepfather was battling his illness and the grief of the passing of his son a few years earlier. Nan told a story of how she felt she had made a difference in a young man's life, someone who had felt he had nowhere to go and no reason to live. *[For that story, see Chapter 1, "The Day the Museum Got Robbed"]* It touched us all, but especially my stepfather, for my stepbrother had taken his life in those earlier years, and my stepfather told her with tears in his eyes that he was so glad she had talked with that young man.

Then he quickly got up on his walker and started walking around outside the store to compose himself, but his walker kept catching on the rocks and finally he just picked it up and started trotting with it.

And all the while Nan was saying, "Someone needs to help him," and then finally saying, "Well, my gosh, he is picking that walker up!"

All we could do was laugh. My stepfather found peace in his heart that day on the porch, and I will always be grateful.

Before we left, Nan took us in the gift shop and showed us around and then she brought out a rag quilt. It was beautiful! I asked her if she sold them and she said, "Yes." When I told her I would take it, I didn't think she believed me. But it was beautiful, absolutely.

And I told her; no one would ever use it, no one! I kept to that promise until February 2012, when I went to the trail ride. I used it to keep warm at the dance and on the porch. Otherwise it has a place of honor in my house.

I came home after that first time meeting Nan, and I started looking for fabric to send out to her. Truth be told, I am responsible for Nan's love of Ebay. I was finding fabric for my sewing on there, and shared that with her, so blame me!

We visited each other over the short number of years after: me and Mother at the store, and Nan, friends and Freddy at my house.

When I am on Stillwell Store's porch, I always name a chair as Robert's chair, in honor of my stepfather. It gives me peace as I sit in it.

God blessed Mother, Robert, and me on September 23, 2006, the day we met Nan and became friends and family. I have always loved the area, but knowing Nan made it so much sweeter.

Luv you, Nan!

29

A WAL-MART ADVENTURE

by Cindy Bolton

Here is another story I have about Nan, but this happened after her passing. I believe she was watching over us! This actually happened July 30, 2012, the day of Nan's memorial service in Marathon.

I wrote to Nan's sister, Kay, and relayed what occurred as follows:

Today Mother and I did our run to Wal-Mart and Sprouts. I am always first finishing; so today I told her I was checking out and putting my things in the jeep, so take your time. As I was putting my stuff in the jeep, which was parked in the handicapped space with Mother's sign hanging in it, I turned around and there was a man waiting for the space. I motioned to him that I was staying. He shook his fist and made faces and raced by as I was practically yelling, "I have to go in and get my Mother!"

I went in and found Mother and told her about it and she said she hoped he didn't come and find me! He didn't.

When Mother is in the grocery area, I lean up against the deep coolers, wait for her, and watch folks. There was an extra-large number of elderly shopping, I am sure from the senior living apartments down the road. I watched one person stop then start talking with a lady who looked to be my age. They talked and both seemed to enjoy their visit. I don't know if they knew each other or what. Soon the elderly lady walked on, and the younger one just looked blank and then started to sob, wiping tears and sobbing. Of course I started to tear up, thinking of Nan, but nothing like this lady. Something was really upsetting her.

I started to walk over, but decided to let her have her time. Soon Mother walked out of the aisle, looked her way, smiled, and said to her, "Oh, there you are again." (Mother had had to move earlier for another lady, but later she realized this wasn't the same person.) Then

Mother walked over to me and we were discussing where to go next in the store.

Out of nowhere, the upset lady came right up to me, hugging my neck and sobbing, so I held her too. She said she lost her mother back in October and she missed her so much and asked if this was my mother. She just held on and sobbed. So I hugged her back and told her she needed a hug. Then I told her I am sure my mother would like to hug her too. (This is kinda out of Mother's comfort zone, but she did it, not hearing what the lady had told me.)

Right there in Wal-Mart, we three were having a hugging fest. We found out the lady's mother's name was Dolores; Mother's name is Doris. The lady's middle name was her mother's first name; my middle name is Doris, my mother's first name. The lady's mother's middle name was Marie; Mother's is Juanita.

We talked more and finally the lady seemed to feel better. She thanked us for the hugs and told me to love the time with my mother.

Mother and I walked off and two aisles over, Mother finally asked, "Who was that?"

I said, "I have no idea, but I will tell you more later." I was sure Mother hadn't heard or seen what I had seen.

As we were walking towards the check out, there was a buggy display with silk flowers for .25 each. I told Mother I wanted to have something to put out at Nan's grave when I go out in November. So we picked out some and proceeded to check out. Nan always said she didn't like receiving fresh flowers. She thought they were a waste of money. So I thought she would approve: fake and cheap. In fact I know she would.

At the checkout a very sweet cashier asked me if these were for a gravesite. I said, "Well, yes, they are!" and told her a little bit about Nan.

She asked if she could give me a hug! And I said, "Sure, and I will give you one too."

Just a few tears leaked out.

She asked if that was my mother, and Mother kinda braced herself. But she didn't hug Mother, but was so, so sweet to her.

Mother paid for her items and we started walking out. I made the comment to Mother, "Do we look pitiful or what??? Everybody is hugging us!"

We both agreed..........it was Nan!

We went on to Sprouts. Nobody hugged us there! But that is ok. Nan didn't know a Sprouts, but she sure knew a Wal-Mart!

30

NAN'S BRUSH WITH FAME

by Tom Petit

See Nan's version of this event in the Chapter 19 Retirement Party story called "Overslept". Here Tom Petit adds a bit more to it...verified by Nan's son, Fred, who said, "Sounds right to me."

Nan was living in Ft. Worth and making the daily commute down I-30 to Dallas with thousands of other people.

There was always lots of construction on I-30. I think at the time they were adding an HOV lane.

Well, one morning Nan is driving to work in heavy traffic and for whatever reason--not paying attention, daydreaming, etc.--she doesn't see that up ahead, her lane is closed and she needs to merge over to another lane.

But the driver next to her isn't letting her in. She keeps driving, thinking she can soon move over. She keeps going and going until her lane ends.

But she doesn't stop--she plows forward and ends up on top of a barricade--her car is up in the air, straddling some concrete barrier. (She said she couldn't make up her mind to go right or left or what, so she just went straight!)

Of course I-30 shuts down and there's a huge traffic jam. Nan is sitting in her car (not injured!) on top of this barrier. She's waiting for help to arrive and listening to the radio.

She hears the traffic report from one of those helicopter reporters. He's laughing about the idiot who caused the huge tie up on I-30 driving.

Nan realizes--hey that's me! Her brush with fame! I think it was even on the evening news because it stopped I-30 for so long.

Nan laughed and laughed about this. She said whenever she heard about some big traffic jam she always remembered the one she caused.

31

THE BUCKET LIST

by Barb and Basil Stewart

My husband and I discovered the Stillwell Ranch and RV Park seventeen years ago on one of our travels to the "West". The Ranch has been a delight.

We so enjoyed the quiet evenings and oh! What sunrises and sunsets! We loved the quiet walks and the rock hunting!

Nan had been a big part of the reason we come back. The tales Nan told added to the excitement of our visit and the experience of the West. The generations of Stillwells proved to be true wild west ranchers.

The Stillwell Ranch was on the "Bucket List" for my 92 year old husband, Basil. *[Since writing this, Barb related that Basil passed away June, 2013.]*

Nan was such a delight to be around. She had the joy for the ranch and RV Park and all the people that visited. She would just "light up" in conversation.

We had the pleasure of visiting Nan on our last days at Stillwell Ranch, and I'm so glad! On our last visit, she still had the "Glow".

32

TURNING THINGS UPSIDE DOWN

by Keith Ritter and Eldon Whitford

We both got to know Nan real well and spent a lot of time with her. Nan had a way of making you feel like you were her best friend. She also had a way of helping you feel comfortable with her warmth, sincerity, charm and her ever-present humor.

During her last winter, her illness had progressed to the point of requiring such life supporting equipment as a feeding tube, an electrically powered oxygen supply and an electric suction wand, as she could no longer swallow (or talk).

One very hot evening, all of the electricity suddenly quit at the ranch. A power supply transformer had blown somewhere many miles away, taking all of the electricity in the northern Big Bend area out.

Keith & Eldon quickly starting hustling for a portable generator to set up, something none of us had made plans for, to power Nan's life support equipment.   Before we got the generator operational, Kay came running out to the shop and said Nan was struggling to breathe.

We both rushed to the store where Nan was lying in a big recliner, looking desperate with real big eyes. We looked at Nan, and she looked back at us with those big eyes. Keith and Eldon looked at each other.

Eldon said, "Nan, we are going to turn you upside down."

She nodded in agreement but her eyes got even bigger. Keith was on one side and Eldon was on the other. We grabbed Nan and lifted her feet to the ceiling. Sure enough, gravity did its job, and Nan started breathing easier.

She also started giggling uncontrollably. So did we. What a silly picture we had created: us standing there, holding Nan with her head to the floor and feet to the ceiling!

Typical of Nan, she was seeing the humor in life's scenarios, even when it was a bit on the tense side.

33

FOURTH OF JULY ENCOUNTER

by Bob Freeman

It was the 4th of July, 2006. We had just bought a home in Marathon, and the tradition here on this holiday is a barbecue down at the county park, Post Park, about 6 miles south of town.

Word was that they served at the pavilion from 11:30 until 2:00, so we headed down there about 1:00 p.m.

Too late. There had been a large wedding in town at the Gage Hotel, and the reception had adjourned to Post Park for barbecue. They had cleaned them out. We were disappointed, to say the least, and it must have shown, because as we headed back to our car to head back to town, a lady approached us, walking awkwardly with a cane. She stopped us, then called to the crew loading up the meat, veggies and pies, and *ordered* them to unpack the food. "You've got to have enough barbecue left in there for two plates!" *No* was just not an acceptable answer.

Sure enough, while the men and ladies grudgingly opened the trays of remaining food and put together two plates heaped high with all the fixin's, we sat and visited with our newly-found advocate. She told us her name was Nan, and that she and her step-dad ran the store and RV Park at the Stillwell Ranch. Turns out, she was waiting for her ride back to town, because she was unable to drive, so she sat and visited as we ate our way into her story. We were familiar with her grandmother, Hallie Stillwell, even though we had never met. Her reputation was the thing of Texas legend, and we felt we were in the presence of royalty. But you would never know it.

From that first meeting, we made it a habit of visiting the Stillwell Ranch, Store and RV Park, at least monthly. Usually, we would ride there, about a 45 mile trip each way, on our motorcycles. My wife, Jodie, is disabled, but she rides her own Harley Davidson trike (a 3-wheel motorcycle), and uses a pair of crutches to walk instead of her wheelchair at the ranch, due to the lack of paved sidewalks or parking area. Even though Nan suffered much of her adult life with disabilities, namely knees and hips, she never complained, and was constantly pulling me aside and whispering to me how great an inspiration that Jodie was to her, not letting her disability slow her down.

Funny, it was Nan and her courage in the face of her terminal illness, that became *our* inspiration, and an example of great courage and positive living to all those who knew her.

Bob and Jodie Freeman

34

THE MUSEUM BREAK-IN

by Bob Freeman

Bob Freeman adds some additional thoughts about Nan's reaction to the theft of guns and money from the museum.

There was the Museum. The Stillwell Museum. It's a wonderful building adjacent to the RV park and general store where ranching and regional memorabilia are preserved for the public to enjoy. No charge. Honor system. Just pick up the key at the Stillwell Store and enjoy a self-guided tour, then return the key.

At some point, not sure what year, there was a breach of trust. A couple of young men opened the museum and stole several of the antique firearms from the display cases. There was no clue as to their identity, since no identification was required to take the key and tour the museum. Honor system.

There were no leads. A dead end. And so, Nan was hurt and frankly, angry, at the breach of trust. However, it did not detour her from continuing to open the museum to all who visited according to their long practice of trust, the honor system, for leaving the artifacts intact and secure for others to enjoy.

I want to say that some two years had passed, and one day a young man walked into the Stillwell Store. He identified himself as the perpetrator of the gun theft, and he wanted to return the guns. He was prepared for his punishment.

Nan looked at us, with moist eyes, and said that she just *knew* that those guns would be returned, and that she just could not prosecute this young man for his honesty. She thanked him for bringing them back, told him how angry she had been at the time of the theft, but how much it meant that he had come clean and shown remorse for his crime, and that she was going to forgive him and send him on his way.

"You just have to have a belief in the basic goodness of people," she said. That's the way she believed, and that's the way she lived.

Richard and Joan Payne

Joan and Nan at a Pioneer Reunion

35

NAN'S EXTRAORDINARY ATTITUDE

by Richard and Joan Payne

The thing I remember most about Nan is the process she lived out with the damnable disease which finally ended her earthly life.

I remember thinking that she wasn't speaking quite clearly; her words were just a bit slurred. It was so minor that I thought maybe I just wasn't listening carefully.

The next thing I knew (we were only at the Ranch for two months each year), Nan had obviously become concerned about her speech and sought out the specialist who famously concluded to Nan that she hadn't had a stroke because she could say both "Methodist" and "Episcopal". *(See Chapter 22, "Radioactive Nan")*

Finally, about our third visit during the time of Nan's difficulties, she got up at the evening "sing and dance" and told her story of going to the Mayo Clinic in Arizona for ten days and how, at the end of those days, she sat down with the specialists who told her she had a serious disease which was terminal and which would gradually rob her of all her faculties, most sadly, her speech.

As sad as that was to hear, Nan's final commentary was the most telling. She simply said, "I was so relieved to know the truth about what was happening to me."

Nan had an extraordinary ability to accept reality and cheerfully and honestly go forth to live each new day. We love her and miss her.

36

RANCH GIRL NAN

by Bob and Gayle Herr

Arriving late in the afternoon at Stillwell Ranch and Store several years ago, we were greeted by a smiling lady, Nan, who enthusiastically guided us to a RV site. We had signed up for two nights; however, we ended up staying five weeks.

Nan's vibrancy and friendliness really "wowed" us. Of course, there were also W.T., Kay, Barbie, Ann and Eldon and others, but Nan set the tone for the whole place.

Her evening storytelling, sitting on the piano bench after the music, was often the highlight of our day - as beautifully expressive as the occasional double rainbow we sometimes saw after a rare rainstorm. In fact at each annual visit we loved hearing some of the same stories again.

Nan told us she enjoyed our homemade scones and muffin treats, but we probably enjoyed "Nan's Burritos" even more. The burritos were oftentimes our supper after the music and storytelling.

Nan shared her love for life and her "ranch girl" heritage with many visitors over the years and we felt like "special friends". We will always remember Nan as our dear friend from West Texas.

Bob and Gayle Herr

**Mary and Ed Rothgarber at Stillwells
2007**

37

AN ADVENTURE WITH NAN

by Mary Rothgarber

I first met Nan at the ranch when she first moved there. Larry was building their house. I had gone to the store to talk and get acquainted. Nan was cooking tapioca pudding and when a customer came in, Nan asked me to stir the pot while she took care of the customer. Well, I guess we bonded then.

We got to talking and she asked if we would be willing to make some sotol walking sticks for the gift shop. She said her friend Lynn Shackelford said to go to the Shackelford Ranch and gather what we needed.

So Nan took an afternoon off from working at the store and away we went, even took our friends, the Zondermans, with us. Nan had a map that Lynn had given her so we knew where to go, as Nan had never been there before.

Well, we missed the ranch driveway and drove all the way to La Linda, which was good since Nan hadn`t been there for years. We eventually found the driveway and followed the map to what we all thought was the right location and gathered a pickup full of sotol poles. They were hanging out the back and dragging on the ground.

The next day Lynn stopped into the store and we discovered we hadn't been on the Shackelford Ranch but on Black Gap property instead! We had a good laugh over that.

The more you went to the ranch the more you loved Nan. She was one of a kind with a heart of gold. She taught me how to make Nan's Burritos and potato bakers. She was a lot of fun and we will all miss her.

I'll never forget her.

Nan and Eldon
2011

38

STILLWELL CAR THIEVES

by Eldon Whitford

This is Eldon Whitford's recollection of one of his favorite stories that Nan used to tell.

Many years ago two vehicles were stolen from the Stillwell Store area in the middle of the night.

They were first alerted to this when they got a call from the Border Patrol, inquiring if they were missing a pickup. It was at Thanksgiving and there were lots of relatives there, so when they gave the description of the vehicles, they checked around and found that, indeed, one was missing. The keys had been left in it. The Border Patrol had captured the "joy riders' and traced the whereabouts of the theft back to Stillwells.

The thieves turned out to be Mexican illegals who must have been tired of walking and decided that borrowing a vehicle sounded like a good idea.

Stillwells soon discovered that their friend's pickup was not the first vehicle these "rustlers" had taken that night. About a half mile down the road was their first choice.

It was an old Stillwell Ranch car, still sitting by the side of the road. The thieves had apparently chosen it first, and pushed it quietly down the road, with the probable intent of hot-wiring it to get it started, once out of earshot of the store. A good car thief is a quiet car thief.

When well out of ear range of the store, they apparently made their attempted start. When nothing happened, they raised the hood to determine what was wrong. The problem was really simple, but very serious: The engine was no longer in the car.

**Barb and Chuck Schneider performing their music
in the museum**

39

BOQUILLAS CHICKEN PARTS CARTEL

by Barb and Chuck Schneider

On one of our earliest visits to the Stillwell ranch, we were playing music with the Whitfords as a warm-up for Nan's storytelling. We were looking for an excuse to sing one of our favorite novelty songs, "CHICKEN".

So, as an introduction Chuck talked about how in the early days there was a yearly cattle drive to Marathon but that left a lot of down time. So, the Stillwells started raising chickens and drove them every six weeks to Marathon.

While we thought this was just a rural fabrication, Nan interrupted and explained that, in fact, the Stillwell Ranch had once been a hotbed of chicken and chicken parts smuggling into Mexico.

Apparently, to protect Mexican chicken producers, high tariffs had been established on chickens and chicken parts (of which the U.S. has an excess of due to our preference for white meat). Therefore, truckloads of frozen chicken parts would routinely stop, sometimes for days, at the ranch. The drivers would wait there for corrupt border guards at Boquillas del Carmen to be in place and ignore the illegal shipments.

To provide a safe house for these Mexican chicken gangs, the Stillwells were paid handsomely in frozen chicken parts. Nan said it was the best fried chicken she ever had.

Amazingly, live chickens were also smuggled across the border, as cock fighting is a major betting venue in Mexico.

Nan shared one occasion where a truckload of fighting roosters spent several days waiting to cross the border. She said that they were too valuable and too tough to eat but that 5 or 6 of them escaped into the desert outside of the ranch. After the truck left, Nan said that it was beautiful to hear them crow in the morning. But, unfortunately, the coyotes didn't know that these roosters were too valuable and too tough. They ate them anyway.   A true story of life and death in the desert.

Sadly, this is another example of where there is high demand for an illicit product, criminal enterprises will provide.   Nan and her family were prime examples of illegal chicken and chicken parts smuggling and its consequences.

Don't let this happen to you!

Barb and Chuck Schneider (Not our real names. We are in the witness protection program.)

40

REMEMBERING NAN

by Mari Bailey-Villanueva

When I retired from Southwestern Bell, I lost track of my dear friend of many years: Nannette Patton, whom I first met in the engineering department at 8800 Broadway in San Antonio. I didn't worry about losing her email address, because we had always agreed that she could ever and always be found through her mom and the Stillwell Ranch association and that she would get back there (from working in downtown Dallas at the time) as soon as she could.

I thus looked forward to her retiring from the telephone company and heading out to Big Bend where we could meet again, as we did for the 4L Centennial and Ms. Hallie's 100th birthday party – two of the most enjoyable and memorable occasions of my life!

She always told people that I had a 'shrine' in my home dedicated to her grandmother, Ms. Hallie, and to this day I think of Nan whenever I look at my 'collection' of Ms. Hallie 'memorabilia'.

That is what prompted my search for Nan today (*winter 2014*) and I am without words to learn that she has passed. Truly the world is a sadder place without her wonderful warm welcoming smile, personality and generous spirit! Oh, how she could make me laugh!

My regret at not having made the effort to find her sooner is enormous. I thus thank whoever took that beautiful portrait of her genuine big smile *[on the Stillwell website]* and then too the 'farewell' hug. They mean a great deal to me.

Nannette always loved the photograph entitled "Hallie's Hands" and it made me smile to see Nan's hands in the 'hug' photo – her hands now also showing the experiences of a life well spent.

Nan, we shall have to meet again at a later date, if I'm lucky enough to find my way to Heaven. I know that you're there, now in your own glory and with your beloved grandmother Ms. Hallie, who is undoubtedly now as proud of you as you always were of her.

**Sande Pedro, standing,
with Nan and Patsy Cavness**

41

RECYCLED EARRINGS

by Sande Pedro

I was not privileged to be a life-long friend of Nan's like many of my friends and neighbors here in Marathon, Texas. I became acquainted with her near the middle of her illness, when she had already lost her gift of speech and the ability to eat and get around much. However, she never lost her love of people or her amazing care and concern or her generosity.

How many of us ever made the "mistake" of exclaiming to Nan how much we liked her earrings? The minute the words left our mouths we were the proud owner of a new pair…as was Nan. She would trade, since you can only wear a pair at a time! I imagine during her lifetime she recycled ten times her original collection, and all in the name of friendship.

She is irreplaceable and sorely missed.

Betty and Tommy Hamilton at a Stillwell campfire

42

OUR VISITS TO STILLWELL STORE AND RV PARK

by Betty and Tommy Hamilton

Sadly, we were late to the "Party" when we discovered Stillwell Ranch Store. Regretfully, we were too late to meet Hallie and Dadie, but others told us about them, and their spirits permeated the air every time we went into the store or gathered around the campfire.

We discovered Stillwell Store and Nan's and Kay's hospitality and the Whitfords' music in late February 2008. We had read the article, "Hallie's Country," in Texas Highways magazine and decided we would drive down and spend the night there. Then we would go on into Big Bend National Park to Rio Grande Village. When we stopped, we told ourselves "one or two nights" only, but we wound up staying a month and would have stayed longer if we could have!

Tommy had gone through a bout of bladder cancer and chemo treatments the previous summer so we had several follow-up tests scheduled. As we registered, we discussed how long we might stay, and in the process explained our reasons for having to get back home for doctors' appointments. When Nan heard about the cancer, she instantly said, "Oh, I'm so sorry. I'll pray for you."

That told us immediately what a loving person she was. When we indicated we weren't sure how long we would stay, probably a "few days," she said she would "run a ticket" and we could just pay when we got ready to leave.

Nan and, if I remember correctly, Ann (or was it Nan's friend Barbie?) were making a batch of "Nan's Meat and Bean" burritos. Having skipped breakfast in Fort Stockton where we had spent the night, as soon as we had the motor home leveled and plugged in, I went back to the store for those delicious burritos. They were a great breakfast – and what an atmosphere for them!

The quiet nights and bright sunny mornings made us so relaxed and worry free, that we felt right at home immediately. Everyone, including visitors, local ranchers, and Nan and family were so friendly and such fun to be around, especially the sitting and visiting on the porch in the evening, that those "few" days very quickly became a little over a month! We reluctantly left, but we had already made plans to return in 2009. The only year we did not get to go was in 2012 because Tommy was recovering from a fractured vertebra and the installation of two stints to his heart. The other years we were able to be at the Stillwell Store for at least a month, usually a little longer than that.

Nan's sense of humor was delightful. Even though she was having a little trouble enunciating and communicating, we readily adapted our ears so that carrying on conversations was easy. She was so cheerful and pleasant to be around that we became unaware of her speech problems until several years later when they had worsened considerably.

Each year that we returned, we were greeted as though we were family. All of us who spent our winters (or a month or more) became as close as siblings, and Nan was the center of it all. Once Tommy decided to get into the "spirit" of "the West" and he began to grow a beard. The first time we saw Nan after his gray beard was thick enough to see, Nan looked at him and said, "What happened, Tommy, did you lose your razor?"

Even though we could tell her health was deteriorating, she never complained and she always had something amusing to say and big hugs when we arrived or departed.

One year, Nan was being honored at the Paisano Hotel in Marfa (Was it her birthday? I don't remember the occasion.) We all decided to drive over there and eat together. We found a nice restaurant with a table large enough to accommodate all of us, and when we finished, we were not allowed to pay for our meal. Nan had already taken care of it!

We learned of Nan's death when we were in New Mexico. We have a "Stillwell Ranch Store" bumper sticker on our pickup and a man told Tommy that Nan had died. We were so sad, but we returned to the Store in the early spring of 2013, and although we missed Nan, her spirit was still evident in the friendly greetings of those who were still there.

43

WE BECAME HAPPY CAMPERS

by Carol Love

About 1997, my sons, James and Lee, my sister Jane, and I went to Big Bend for the first time. We couldn't get into the national park to camp because it was full. So we ended up going back to the Stillwell Ranch to camp.

I was not a happy camper and didn't want to stay there but we had no choice!

We have been coming back every year since! We only missed one year in the years to follow.

Nan was always the one to draw us back! She would fuss at the boys when they were climbing the trees or doing flips on the hitching post in front of the store! They loved to surprise her when they would come back for spring break. Lee even helped to wait on tables one spring break when Wally *[a noted chuck wagon cook]* was there serving chuck wagon food to the campers.

Nan and W.T.

44

LIKE COMING HOME

by Jane Spakes

I'm Jane Spakes, sister to Carol Love. *[See Chapter 43, "We Became Happy Campers".]* I have been coming to Stillwell Ranch as long as my sister and nephews have. I would like to argue that it was earlier than 1997, but she is the oldest and I'll let her have this one.

Not being able to camp in Big Bend was heartbreaking, but only for a moment. Arriving at Stillwell and being welcomed by Nan was one of the best things that could have happened to us. We have been coming back to Stillwell ever since. Even today, Spring Break 2014, Nan's welcoming spirit is still there.

Coming back to Stillwell each year was and is like coming home. My husband, Jim, has been returning each year with me since before we were married. We always wanted Nan to come up to our camp for dinner, but because of the store hours, she couldn't make it. So we brought dinner to her, her dad (W.T.), and all that were working at the store. Nan loved my Korn-Koction (recipe follows). It is a little something that I came up with while camping at Mt. Rushmore with Jim and the Loves.

We learned a lot from Nan through the years. Her storytelling of her grandmother Hallie's adventures brought the past back to life. Her love of the museum was evident. Each time new folks came to the store, she made sure to tell them about the museum. Nannette was such a trusting soul. Although the museum was locked, she always gave the key to anyone who wanted to visit it. That for me, coming from Houston at the time, was just amazing. I locked everything!

Getting to know her dad, W. T. was an adventure in itself. He was a typical stoic Marine with a dry sense of humor. He was a quiet man until you got to know him, which didn't take long. Only about 10 years!

My husband, a retired Marine, gave us a way in. He and W.T. had a lot to share. W.T. was a World War II Marine, and Amtrak driver who was in the first wave on Iwo Jima. We were both amazed by him. Our last Spring Break with W.T. manning the store, we will never forget. He took us to his home and shared his memorabilia and stories with us. We felt like we had finally made it to the "inner circle."

One of our favorite stories we like to tell of W.T. is when he had a new camper come in to the store and ask if it was OK to have a campfire. W.T. told him, "Yea, but keep it small…3 to 5 acres."

With the passing of W.T. and Nan, another era of Stillwell has closed. We sincerely hope that a new era is beginning and the history, love of the land and Hallie Stillwell, will continue to be passed on to future generations of Texans and all who visit the 4L.

Korn-Koction

1 stick butter
1 onion, diced to a size you like
1 potato, diced
1 can corn
1 can Mexi corn
fajita seasoning (if not available, use pepper, garlic and a little salt)
crushed red pepper, to taste (Korean red pepper paste is preferred, but hard to find)

Using a skillet, throw in the butter, onion, potato and seasonings. Cook it up. When the onions have softened and the potatoes are cooked, add the corn. Add additional seasonings to taste. The Korn-Koction is done when the corn is thoroughly heated.

The fun thing about this recipe is it never comes out the same way twice. I just shake in the seasonings. If you don't like spicy, leave out the red pepper. Experiment: try more corn, green and red bell pepper, some green onions (some people call them scallions). Canned potatoes work great too. Enjoy!

45

THE SECRET WE SHARED

by Keith Ritter

In the late winter of 2012, Nan's physical condition had deteriorated so much that she could no longer drive. Though she spent her days at the store, she still insisted on staying at her own house at night. That meant that someone needed to drive her there, and then pick her up every morning.

One morning I went into the store about 9 a.m., an hour after it opened, looked around and noticed Nan wasn't there. So I asked Kay, "Where's Nan?"

"Oh crap!" she replied. "I forgot to get Nan! Would you take her truck and go get her?"

So I drove to Nan's house, about a half mile from the store via a curving dirt road. When I got there, I knocked on the door. No answer.

Now we all knew that Nan's health was quickly going south. She was no longer able to eat because she couldn't swallow. She was taking liquids through a tube in her stomach. Because she couldn't swallow, she couldn't keep saliva from filling her throat, so she had a suction tube she used to clear her mouth and throat. By then she was also on oxygen because her lung muscles were beginning to fail, too. So, her health was precarious, and we all knew anything could happen to her at any time.

So when she didn't answer my knock at the door, my heart started beating faster. I went around to all the windows, looking in, afraid of what I'd see. I couldn't see her anywhere. What to do?

Then I thought…her house key is probably on the key ring with her truck keys. Sure enough, I found a key to fit the lock and entered the house, calling out her name. Still no answer. My heart was pounding by this time, as I walked through the side room towards the main part of her house, calling for her. Finally I heard a faint sound…it was Nan!

There she was in the doorway between her bedroom and living room. She had fallen there, wearing only her underwear, and hadn't been able to get up. I found out later that she had lain there all night. I rushed over to her, and she flashed a big grin. She couldn't help lift herself at all, so I reached down with a big bear hug, and lifted her up. She just kept grinning.

I left her to get dressed and she soon came out with her white board and marker. She had written, "You are the only person who has ever seen me naked!" We both laughed.

On the way back to the store in her truck, she wrote, "Don't tell anyone!" She didn't want Kay to find out, because she knew that Kay wouldn't want her to stay alone at her house anymore. I promised I wouldn't tell.

But when we got back, I just had to tell someone. So I told Eldon *[Whitford],* and swore him to secrecy too. So Kay didn't find out about that fall.

A few weeks later, a whole group of us were sitting on the porch, as we often did at Stillwell. Nan and I were side by side on a double rocker. She had her white board with her, and wrote again, "Remember, you promised not to tell!" We both chuckled over our secret again.

If you ever see the DVD "On the Porch" and wonder about the sequence of photos with Nan and me on the porch that day, smiling and laughing at one another, that's the big secret we were sharing.

Nan made me promise not to tell until she had passed. I guess she wouldn't mind me telling about it now.

Keith and Nan chuckling about their secret

46

NAN'S BIRTHDAY LETTER

Knowing that Nan would be having her last birthday in July of 2012, many of us sent her cards and letters. Here is mine…

Dear Nan-

First of all, HAPPY BIRTHDAY TO YOU!!!   I wish I could be there in person to tell you all I want to say. This letter will have to do.

I want to tell you how much your friendship has meant to me. You might not remember the first time we talked, but I do. I called the store (from Michigan) to see if you might be interested in having some music as part of your evening program. You were so polite, and gave your usual, "Come on down...I can hardly wait for you to get here!" but of course, made no promises about us doing music. You didn't even know us!

So, with no promises made or expectations on our part, we drove back down to Big Bend, checked in, and came in to do a couple of songs for you. I don't remember if there were other people there in the store or not, but when we played a couple of songs, we were in! (: Thus was the beginning of Live Music at Stillwell's.

Not only did we play music, but you quickly took us in as friends, and soon we were "in the kitchen", helping in the store, and getting to know you, as you were getting to know us.

If it hadn't been for YOU, we never would have been able to become a part of the Stillwell family. I can't imagine what our retired lives would have been without our home-away-from-home at Stillwell's. Being your warm-up act in the evening at the museum was fun as well as great experience for us musically. You inspired us to record our first "real" CD, "Goin' Back to Stillwell Mountain", and of course, you launched Eldon's (short but sweet) song-writing career when he wrote "Nan's Burritos". I doubt we would have become the musicians we are today without all those evening programs at the Hallie Stillwell Hall of Fame.

You are the best story-teller I know, and the best friend as well. I treasure the many times spent with you...at the store, on the porch, during our travels to Alpine and beyond, talks in our camper, your visit here in Michigan...all are such special memories. We had seven (or is it eight?) wonderful winters, and I feel so blessed to have had all that time with you. Of course, I expected the fun times to continue for many more years, and am crushed that we won't have all that additional time together....at least not on this earth.

If I get a chance to see you in another time and place, I will know what to look for: a porch, probably with you seated in a comfortable rocking chair, surrounded by your adoring fans. You, perhaps with a Dr. Pepper in hand, will be telling another story; they'll all be laughing and begging for more. That's something to really look forward to!

I love you, Nan!

Your friend forever,
Ann

**Uhl and Nancy Donovan at Stillwells
2007**

47

THE LADY CALLED NAN

by Uhl Donovan

I don't remember the first time we met Nan Patton, one of four granddaughters of Hallie Stillwell. I just remember the pleasant smile, the sparkling eyes, and the invitation to friendship.

Our first trip to Stillwell was in the spring of 2000. We had just missed Hallie. Dadie *[Nan's mother]* was the "trail boss," Johnny was the hired hand, and W.T. had been given orders to stay in the trailer. Guy *[brother to Dadie]* was also at the ranch at that time.

Our stay was short in 2000, so we didn't get too well acquainted but we decided to return the following year. There was something about this brush-covered, waterless, one-time cattle ranch that drew us back to Stillwell and Hallie's Hall of Fame.

The spring of 2001 had to be our first introduction to Nan. Before then, Dadie had given nightly a short introduction before we watched, "Change in the Bend" (*a DVD about the Stillwells and life in the Big Bend area of West Texas*) in the museum. Now, Dadie had cashed in, W.T. was the new boss, and his sidekick was Nan.

Nancy and I had had several conversations with Nan about the ranch and RV Park and we saw firsthand the importance of volunteers. Each night we would learn more about the history of Stillwell. One night Nan, perched on the piano bench, told us about Hallie's first cattle drive to Marathon. On the first day of the drive, Hallie, wanting to be a helpful part of the crew, struggled with an old cow that would break from the herd and go south. All day, Hallie kept riding out to bring her back, only to be told by Roy after several retrieves, "Oh, let her go, Hallie. If you had looked close, you'd see she doesn't even have our brand. Her bag and udders tell you she is nursing a calf, and you keep bringing her back to the herd."

When the ranch hands settled for the first overnight rest, there was a small shack that the crew used. Roy boiled up several buckets of water and poured the hot water over the cracked floor of the shack.

Hallie said, "Roy, if you had wanted to clean the floor, we could have scrubbed it with the broom."

Roy's reply was, "Hell, I'm not cleaning the floor. I'm trying to settle down the skunks and rattlesnakes under it!"

That was the second of many insults that Hallie experienced with her new home and life at the ranch.

Nan had a special way of placing you into the many stories that she would tell of Stillwell. Many of these stories were put into Hallie's books, "I'll Gather My Geese" and "My Goose is Cooked."

Nan loved her Stillwell family and she wanted others to experience this rich history and the many struggles endured with keeping the land.

Our special times with Nan soon suggested that we could become volunteers and help other people enjoy the riches of Stillwell. We returned for several seasons to help with the trail rides, spring break, and to do several improvements to the ranch.

I told Nan that I could rebuild the left stone column across from the store. It had been knocked down by a jerk who drove an RV through the gate, hit the cross bar, and took out the cross bar and left column. Believe it or not, he was mad at the staff for not telling him about the possibility that his RV wouldn't fit under it. Kay's husband, David, was a superb hod carrier (a mortar mixer and go-fer for a stone mason) as well as a wonderful helper with that and many other projects. He and Kay were delightful people to work and visit with.

When Dadie passed away, W.T. pretty much ran the ranch. He was pretty tight fisted, and didn't want to spend money to fix up the place. Nan and I would think of projects to do to make the RV campers' visits more enjoyable, only to have the plans nixed by the head boss. Often times, Nan would be driven to tears when W.T.'s disapproval ended with, "All you want to do is spend, spend, spend!"

Well, time went on. We and many others would take the five mile drive down Highway 2627 to "the cut" in the road at the top of the hill. There you could see the ranch and know that good times were about to happen. This became a family reunion to all of us.

We would visit, tell lies, and have a cold drink around a campfire after listening to "The Whitfords" play music in the museum. On many occasions we would enjoy a Dutch oven treat following the music and dancing. Dadie had her crew add the concrete patio to

Hallie's Museum because she wanted her visitors to have a place to dance, to enjoy and remember their stay.

Wally and the trail riders also became an important annual event. To enjoy a meal that Wally prepared with his mobile chuck wagon was unforgettable.

You see, all of this was a product of Nan and her volunteer staff, W.T., sister Kay, friend Barbie, and so many others who knew their efforts would "gel" these happenings into unforgettable memories.

All good things seem to end before we are ready to give them up. Health problems began to make Nan's life not so enjoyable, but you couldn't detect all of the agony because of the positive nature of this remarkable person.

As Nan's health began to interfere with her management duties, sister Kay became the main driving force to keep Stillwell alive. She moved to the ranch, though she was separated from her family in San Antonio. Good friend Barbie was also just one step behind Nan and Kay during their years as COB (Chairwomen of the Board).

W.T.'s passing made work more taxing for Kay, who said that with Nan's emotional and physical deterioration, she (Nan) turned into W.T., with the familiar, "All you want to do is spend, spend, spend!" now directed at Kay.

Nan was an unforgettable individual. Her physical handicap did nothing to slow her down, to alter her rich sense of humor, her vibrant personality, and her ability to rivet you to your chair during her story-telling time, whether in the museum or on the porch at Stillwell.

We will miss her!

48

NAN AND STILLWELL

by Lynne Morse

Lynne Morse's memories of Nan are all entangled with memories of time spent at Stillwell...so here they all are:

- Sitting on the porch with Nan and having a great time telling stories. Plus, you could walk over any time and sit in the store chatting with Nan, Kay, Barbie, WT, locals, friends or relatives who were around. Every person I met at the store was willing to give you a big smile and wish you a happy day, even though sometimes I had to work on WT.

- The locals were a hoot—as soon as they got to know you, they treated you with respect (with lots of crazy humor added also) and I always looked forward to seeing everyone again the next time I'd visit.

- Sitting by the campfire "yucking it up" with everyone.

- Nan coming in to the museum and eyeing Gary (my husband) to get him to dance with her, even though he doesn't want to dance, and then if she had already told her stories, she'd get up, motion him to get over and dance with her to the great music Ann and Eldon were playing

- Nan's wonderful, wonderful stories, and as soon as I began to hear them, I just kept laughing and laughing; especially the one with Freddy and the window…

- Gary taking garbage out late at night wearing only his underwear, assuming all our camping friends would be in bed (and the last time he did that there was a bear in our campground in northern Wisconsin); meanwhile, Richard and Joan pull in with their car lights nice and bright catching Gary in the act. We all had a great laugh over that and I still wonder why those two were out so late.

Gary and Lynn Morse at a Stillwell campfire

- Meeting Freddy at the memorial service for Nan and his comment in tears, "I didn't have a clue how many special friends my mom had made in all these years." I gave him a big hug and a kiss, and said, "It was good for you to experience this as these memories, as well as the memories you had growing up will give comfort to you now and in the future; and this is a lesson in life to experience the joy of living every day."

- There was a calmness and uniqueness around Stillwell that is very fascinating to me. It was as if I was in a different time period and just happened to land in a remote spot in Texas where everyone made you feel special—as if no matter who you talked to, what you said, whether you laughed or cried, the friends and travelers who may have just been stopping by for a quick camp spot before going into Big Bend National Park— made the beauty of Stillwell.

- When Nan passed, I wrote a couple of comments on the Stillwell web page as follows: Nan, you always had that gleam in your eye whenever you were ready to get Gary out dancing—I'll sure miss all the laughs and great stories we shared. You have a very special place in my heart and I will miss you dearly. You were truly a delight to be around and you made our stay at Stillwell very special. All the fun stories by the campfire and in the museum will be cherished…And I know you'll be watching from somewhere to ensure we're having a great time kicking our heels to the music and adventures at the ranch.

- I had a great feeling to be able to experience Stillwell—I felt the environment was so precious that I had both my children come and experience with awe some of the feelings I had over the years. Pam and Stephen came first as they lived in Texas at the time, and I remember Stephen saying he never experienced so many people being so kind to him. Then while we were at Big Bend (the park) after they arrived, he said it was time to get back so we could enjoy the music at the museum because he had such a good time. We paid for Tom to fly in from Durham, NC, while he was working on his PhD. He also thoroughly loved meeting all our friends, chatting with everyone and going to the museum to listen to the music. And when we all talk about Stillwell now, we have such wonderful memories of all the people who made it special to each of us.

49

MISSING NAN AND HER BURRITOS

by Darlene and Roger Boyer

We just thought so much of Nan. She had such a sweet spirit. She always was so happy to see us and everyone else when we arrived and then was sad to see us leave. She always had a smile.

We enjoyed hearing her stories of her grandmother and of her and her sister Kay. It's so hard to believe that they are all gone.

It was a joy to see Nan light up when the Whitfords would sing about her burritos. The burritos were really good and we miss them. I tried to make some but they weren't like Nan's. I should have asked her for the recipe.

Darlene and Roger Boyer

50

QUIETLY KIND

by Mark Kirtley

Mark lived in one of the rentals at Stillwells for a period of time while working at Big Bend National Park. An expert in many areas, he is especially known for his presentation on birds and bird songs, as well as loving to dance.

Mostly I have memories of Nan as quietly kind. Like when she and I and Kay and David played Hearts at her house, she made sure we were supplied with popcorn even though her disease was advanced enough that she could not talk.

Or a moment in the backroom of the store, some years earlier, she and I were sitting and talking at the table. She was assembling some crafty objects to be sold at the store, stringing beads and crocheting. She showed me how to make them with a calmness that helped me to have fun. She gave me some yarn, beads, and even (I think) a crochet needle to take with me so that I could do it on my own if I wanted.

**Mark dancing with Barbie Maher
on the dance floor beside the museum
2011**

Barbie Maher

51

MY WONDERFUL HELPER

by Barbie Maher

Barbie and Nan worked together in Dallas at the telephone company. They remained life-long friends. After her retirement, Barbie spent many months at Stillwells each year, where she became Nan's right-hand helper in the store and kitchen, and a friend to many of the Stillwell "regulars".

During the time Nan and I were roommates, she helped me get through a very trying time in my life. My mom was beginning to go through changes in her personality because of Alzheimer's. Mom had moved into the house across the street from my house. She spent evenings with us watching TV.

One night we were watching "Judging Amy", when all of a sudden Mom got up and motioned me to the kitchen. She started complaining about Nan. I can't remember what it was about.

Later, after Mom had gone home, Nan said all she could hear was, "NAN, blah,blah,blah, NAN, blah,blah,blah, NAN, blah,blah,blah."

We laughed about it. I know for a fact Nan's wonderful sense of humor got me through many, many trying times.

**Heather, Josh, and Abby Whitford with Nan
in the Stillwell Store Gift Shop in 2011**

52

THE ICING ON THE CAKE

by Heather Whitford

Josh & I had been hearing about Stillwell's from Ann & Eldon (Whitford) for quite a while and had finally decided to take a road trip down there. They described it as being "very remote" and "out in the middle of nowhere," so for our initial trip down there, we had only set aside 3 days to visit. We were thinking we would get bored. Our intention primarily was to visit Ann & Eldon at this place they loved so much.

Upon arriving, we pretty much immediately regretted the decision to only stay for 3 days. It was incredible and we instantly fell in love with Stillwell's.

It's very hard to put it all into words, but the people there were so welcoming and friendly that we right away felt at home. The view was amazing and we couldn't have asked for a more beautiful setting.

Then to put the icing on the cake we met Nan, and upon meeting her, never wanted to leave. She had that personality that drew people to her. She just lit up a room. She truly cared about each and every person she met and went out of her way to make everyone feel welcome. She was that person that you consider family even after just spending a few hours with her. You just knew she would forever become part of your life.

Her stories never failed to brighten our day and burn memories into our minds forever. Her stories are part of what we will miss most about her. Storytelling was probably one of her most endearing traits.

Nan was loved by anyone who was fortunate enough to meet her and become part of her life. She was what brought everyone back every year to Stillwell's. We very much looked forward to that atmosphere and especially seeing her. I just can't say enough how incredibly amazing of a person she was.

She was family & we will forever miss our Radioactive Nan.

Nan dancing with Dutch Zondervan

53

LEARNING THE TEXAS TWO-STEP

by Dutch and Bonny Zondervan

The first time that we came to the Stillwell Ranch was in 2004 and that is how we met Nan. It was our first RVing adventure camping out in our minivan.

Nan always had a sparkle in her eye and was a great storyteller about her life experiences on and off the ranch.

My most memorable experience of Nan was when she was teaching me to dance the Texas Two-Step with the wonderful music performance of Ann and Eldon Whitford.

This past year we visited the Stillwell ranch *(2014)* but it is not the same without Nan.

When far west Texas thoughts are on our minds, we think of Nan, doing chores like making burritos for the Spring Break college geology students, moving cars and canoe trailers and finding sotols (*see Mary Rothgarber's story in Chapter 37*) to make walking sticks to be sold in the gift shop.

The Whitfords composed a song about Nan's Burritos that was sung just about every time when they performed.

We have fond memories of Nan and the Stillwell ranch.

Rochelle and Doug Hippen at a Trail Ride BBQ

54

A BEAUTIFUL QUILT OF STILLWELL MEMORIES

by Rochelle and Doug Hippen

Our first impression of the Stillwell Trailer Camp was not a good one. This particular March afternoon was very hot and miserable, but over the years we had heard a lot of "talk" about the Stillwells. So we were anxious to see for ourselves the newly opened Hallie's Hall of Fame Museum. But when we arrived, we found the place totally deserted.

There was a broken pay phone on the porch and through the open screen door was an old-fashioned store. It was stocked with dusty VHS movies, books, souvenirs, a lot of snack food items, and even a mail rock. RV hook-ups were $11.00! An old man soon shuffled out and handed over the key to the museum.

Neither one of us felt very safe or comfortable, so Doug volunteered to stand guard at the door while I went inside. It was cool, dark, and silent. There were old photos, newspaper articles, arrowheads, antique furniture, artifacts, and many other relics from the bygone days of early Stillwell. I found the museum spectacular!

We walked back to the store and left the key on the counter. The last thing we wanted was to be caught out after dark in such a desolate place.

I wanted to go back to Stillwell several times, but Doug would say, "Why the hell would you want to go back to that dump?" But I always felt that the simplicity and remoteness of Stillwell were part of its appeal.

It would be several years later before we returned. On this trip, we were in our motor home and planned to stay overnight. As we crossed through the Gap at the top of the hill overlooking the RV park, we both gasped, as there were people and horses everywhere. We had crashed the annual February Trail Ride!

Again the old man was there and told us, "There's only two spots left, so go out and pick one!"

When we returned to the store counter, a young lady emerged from a crevice of a kitchen and introduced herself. "Hi, I'm Nan." And that's when all the fun really began!

Over the years we grew to love Stillwell and Nan. She liked to dance and often saved one for Doug. She was always smiling and full of joy—enjoying the simple life. Night after night her humorous stories came alive in the museum. She embroidered some, left out a stitch now and then, but overall she sewed a beautiful quilt of Stillwell memories to her audiences. People came from all over to hear her storytelling.

Following in her pioneer grandmother's footsteps, Nannette will someday become a well-known legend in Big Bend country. We love you, Nan! Happy "tales" to you…until we meet again.

55

A SOUL MATE CALLED NAN

by Nancy Donovan

"True Love's the gift which God hath given,
To man alone beneath the heaven.
The silver link, the silver tie,
Which heart to heart, and mind to mind,
In body and in soul can bind."
-Sir Walter Scott

What are the chances of so many, many people, from all across the country, knowing this woman called Nan, and having had a deep relationship with her? Life seems to be a great gamble – is it the "roll of the dice" or divine intervention? The greatness of time and space, compared to our tiny existence has puzzled all of mankind. We pass by many places and by many people, all judged by us, according to our mood, situation, and perception at that time. Why are some situations common or routine, while some people and places are very unique or almost mythical to us? Why is this lady, this family, this place called Stillwell so special? Why is Nannette and why is the Stillwell Ranch?

We came thirteen years ago just needing a place for the night, and were planning to see only the Big Bend National Park. Dadie and Linda were here the first two years. Then we met Nan at the store. She had just retired. She was in charge, with her duty to save the land, save the ranch, and be the one Stillwell to hang on until the next one stepped in to succeed her. She had in mind this most special trust and she did her part with great joy and energy.

As we got acquainted and listened to Nan, we could see that the assignment she had undertaken was a very tall order. There seemed to be only limited "worker bees" in sight. We discussed how we might be of help, came to an agreement, and kept in touch because so much planning was necessary in the off season. She made a list of possible projects each year, and we did many odd jobs, some more odd than others, including a great variety of repairs, new inventions, and cleaning. Our relationship grew over the next ten years.

As the beauty of the area draws certain people, so did Nan. She had a very bright mind, a very big heart, unlimited humorous stories on two levels; hers, and of folks past. Within the giver and the receiver, she could produce much hearty laughter, as well as multitudes of subtle smiles and within our understanding, or misunderstanding, of her gestures.

Nan was an all-around beautiful person. She was handed two extreme physical difficulties; one at birth for her to deal with throughout her life, and the other that later took her life. She worked with them both, struggling with one daily, fighting with the other for every breath during her final months of life. She worked bravely, carrying on, a strong, strong trooper.

After she became unable to talk, she became very adept in communicating with people via her writing pad, hand gestures, and facial expressions. She remained interested in politics, people, spirituality, and loved jokes. She definitely exhibited holy hospitality, a life-giving force, the presence of God, vivacious and enthusiastic, good hearted and loving.

We always enjoyed her transient admirers and were thankful to have met many of the family, and her many, many friends and campers. The winter Texans that came to love her and the ranch have recently been marked with a special brand: the Stillwell Groupies. We could say that they are a powerful determined bunch, especially when the Groupies could get Nan all the way to Minnesota and Michigan for a grand reunion. We often talked about her traveling to our various homes so that we could return her favor of hospitality. Her presence was such a treat that several from other states made sure to stop on their way through just to join in the fun. These special folks, with Nan being the center -- The Prez, Big Cheese, or Head Guru -- will always remain close and be known as the "Stillwell Cult" or "RV Ghetto-ites." Historically speaking, they were the "Hang around the Fort Stillwell Folk." So you see, Nan attracted all kinds. Whether they knew it or not, or felt it or not, there was a very trusting higher relationship than existed at just any RV park.

By contributing to this project, we are memorializing the testament of friendship that started with the Stillwell pioneers, thrived through Nan, and continues to this day. The resulting association of folks across the American landscape because of Nan, encompasses the total truism of freedom, with the love and beauty of our national individual lives, and of those we meet along the way. We all have backgrounds as special as the people we meet, and the landscape and experience that have molded them. Over a period of time, this variety of many different people and backgrounds is marked and hardened together in a single solid group of loving and caring for Nan and the Stillwell family. Through the great distances of our lives, we are together in our love and thankfulness for Nan.

How could a person and a place become so dear as Nan and the Stillwell ranch? Maybe that is why the experience came to be, even though it was not sought after… It was one of those few "wow" experiences that happen so rarely in one's lifetime. We loved her and always will, remaining thankful for experiencing the Big Bend area, the residents, the history, and the family. A Soul Mate called Nan, was a Soul Mate to all.

A favorite gathering place—the Stillwell kitchen table
From left, Nan, Ann Whitford, Barbie Maher, Rosie Potter, and
Kay Pizzini

PART III

NAN'S FAVORITE RECIPES

NAN'S FAMOUS BURRITOS

Thanks to Nan's friend, Barbie Maher, for this recipe. Barbie continued to make them at Stillwells after Nan couldn't. These burritos were very popular, and even have a song written about them (see facing page)...

1 1/2 lbs. ground chuck or hamburger meat
1 medium onion, diced
2 cloves garlic, minced
Jalapeno slices, diced or 2 or 3 tsps. juice
1 pkg. taco seasoning
pinto beans, 3 cups (cooked) plus juice/broth
4 medium potatoes, diced
cheddar cheese, grated
2 pkgs. flour tortillas
Salt and pepper to taste

Cook beans as usual. (Nan used to do a large batch in the crock pot overnight.) Dice onion, mince garlic and add to meat and brown in a large, deep skillet. Scoop out some of the excess fat. Add diced jalapenos and the juice. Add 3 cups of beans with liquid to the meat mixture. Stir in the taco seasoning and mix well. Set aside.

Fry potatoes in about 2 or 3 tbsp. Crisco. Then add to meat mixture.

Open bag of tortillas and heat in microwave for 1 minute, then turn bag over and heat additional 30 or 40 seconds to soften and make them "rollable". Fill each tortilla with about 1 1/2 tbsp. of meat mixture, top with some grated cheese and roll tortilla burrito style.

Serve with salsa and/or jalapeno slices on the side, if desired.

Can be refrigerated or frozen to enjoy later. Just pop in the microwave for a minute or two.

Enjoy!

Nan's Burritos*

(A Musical Tribute to Nan's Burritos)
by Eldon and Ann Whitford

Have you tried Nan's Burritos?
Jalapeno bean burritos?
For they are the best in the land (Yum! Yum!)
Once you've eaten Nan's Burritos,
You won't be bitten by mosquitos.
They're the hottest thing this side of the Rio Grande.

Jalapeno bean burritos…your belly is El Nino!
Once you've had one, you'll want some more.
So get more of Nan's Burritos, with a side of jalapenos.
You can only get 'em at the Stillwell Store.
Y'All come and get 'em at the Stillwell Store!

*as recorded on "Goin' Back to Stillwell Mountain"

NAN'S TOMATO PIE

1 pie crust
10-15 roma tomatoes
1 tsp. salt
1 c. mozzarella cheese (grated)
1 c. pepper jack cheese (grated)
1 c. cheddar cheese (grated)
1 c. Hellmann's mayo
1 bunch of green onions (chopped)

Blind bake the crust until lightly brown. Then let it cool while you prepare the filling.

Blanch the tomatoes by placing them quickly in boiling water, and then ice water. Remove the skins and seeds, and dice them. Place the chopped tomatoes in a colander and sprinkle with about 1 tsp. salt, which will help release the liquid. Let them sit about 30 minutes to drain thoroughly.

Mix together the mayo and 3 cheeses. Chop the green onions.

Then assemble the pie: Place the well-drained tomatoes in the crust first. Top with the cheese mixture, spreading to seal the edges. Top with the green onions.

Bake at 375 until the cheese is melted and lightly brown…about 20 minutes. Cool a bit, then serve. Best served warm.

That might be a tomato pie just coming out of the oven

**Barbie Maher and Mary Lou Rothgarber
in the Stillwell kitchen**

**Nan demonstrates the art of making
Cheese and Onion Enchiladas to Mary Sievert**

142

CHEESE AND ONION ENCHILADAS

Nan said she learned to make these from her mom, Dadie.

½ stick butter
¼ c. flour
2 cans red enchilada sauce (15 oz.), preferably Hatch's medium
1 can tomato soup (10 ¾ oz.)
24 corn tortilla shells
1 ½ c. chopped onions
6 c. shredded cheese (½ colby, ½ pepperjack)

Melt butter in a saucepan. While stirring over medium heat, whisk in flour to make a roux. Whisk in the two cans of enchilada sauce. It will thicken slightly. Whisk in the tomato soup as well. Heat thoroughly while stirring. Remove from heat.

Fry corn shells in hot oil, turning once, just long enough to cook slightly, but still be pliable (about 20 seconds total). Drain on paper towels.

Spray two large baking pans with sides (a broiler pan, or cake pan works as well) with cooking spray.

For each pan, assemble the 3-layered enchiladas as follows: Dip each shell in the sauce and place in the pan, not touching. (Your pan should hold either 4 or perhaps 6 shells.) Sprinkle each with approximately ¼ c. cheese and 1-2 T. chopped onions. Add a second and third layer of dipped shells, again sprinkling each layer with cheese and onions. Add extra sauce as desired.

Bake at 375 for 10-15 minutes until the cheese is bubbly and enchiladas are heated through.

Makes 8 (3-layer) enchiladas. For smaller portions, do only 2 layers per enchilada.

Serve w/shredded lettuce and a slice of tomato on the side.

SOPAPILLA CHEESECAKE

3 large pkgs. cream cheese, softened
1 c. sugar
juice of 1 lemon
zest from that lemon
2 pkgs. Crescent rolls
1 stick butter

Topping: ½ c. sugar, 2 tsp. cinnamon

Cream together: cream cheese, sugar, lemon juice, and lemon zest until smooth.

Spray a 13x9 pan w/Pam. Spread one package crescent rolls and press together to form bottom crust in pan.

Spread cream cheese mixture over bottom crust layer.

Top with other package crescent rolls.

Melt butter and pour over top. Mix topping of sugar and cinnamon and sprinkle over top.

Bake at 350 approximately 30 minutes until nicely browned.

Chill before serving.

Nan at 6 months old

PART IV

MORE PHOTOS
of
FAMILY AND FRIENDS

At about age 5

Riding bicycle

All smiles at about age 10

The Four Sisters
from left, Linda, Nan, Marlene, and Kay

Probably Nan's High School Graduation Photo

150

Nan at her son's wedding – October 27, 2001
Fred and Robin Patton

Nan with 5 year old granddaughter, Abby

Nan and her son, Fred

Nan sharing a story and a laugh with Uhl Donovan – 2007

**A favorite pastime—sitting on the porch at Stillwells
From left: Nan, Eldon Whitford, unidentified camper, W.T., and
Megan O'Neill Coyan (2008)**

Mike Boren and Nan at a Pioneer Reunion
Big Bend National Park

Nan with the Whitfords after music in the museum

One of Nan's favorite times was during campfires at Stillwells…

Nan and David Moffitt

Keith Ritter tending the fire

Eldon Whitford and Gary Morse

Nan, Barbie, and Kay sharing a laugh

**From left: John and Pam Vawter, Rochelle Hippen,
Barbie Maher, and Kay Pizzini**

Richard and Joan Payne at a Stillwell Campfire

Another favorite event for Nan was the Stillwell BBQ Dance held during the annual trail ride in February…

Nan and Macky Shackelford

Nan and Dene Halvorson

Nan with Isabel Nielsen in Michigan
Isabel and her husband were longtime Stillwell campers.

**Carol Dunn created this photo of Nan during Nan's visit
to Michigan in August of 2010**

Bob and Gayle Herr with Nan in the museum

One of the annual New Year's Eve parties held at Stillwells. This one was in 2011. Nan is in one rocker. Jodie Freeman is in the other.

David and Janet Paul
Frequent Stillwell campers from South Dakota

Bernard and Judi Calhoun
at the Stillwell Trail Ride 2010

The view from the hilltop during a busy time at Stillwells

An evening music program in the museum

**Nan's sister, Kay, with Nancy Donovan
at Nan's Celebration of Life February 2, 2013**

**Nan's casket at her graveside service in Marathon, TX
She selected and designed it herself.**

The stone marking her grave

ABOUT THE EDITOR

Ann Whitford was born and raised in rural Michigan. She taught middle school for 31 years before retiring in 2003. She has been married to Eldon Whitford since 1967. They have three children and three grandchildren.

In retirement, Ann & Eldon perform as "The Whitfords," playing traditional country music in Michigan as well as across the U.S. They perform as a duo, as well as in a band, as noted on their website, www.thewhitfordsmusic.com.

Since discovering the Big Bend area of West Texas in 2004, they have spent winters there, performing for the campers and tourists near Big Bend National Park. Over the years of playing at the Hallie Stillwell Hall of Fame, they grew attached to the Stillwell family, enjoying the friendship and camaraderie of Nan, Kay, and all the other Stillwell "regulars". It was this friendship with Nan that led to Ann's promise to Nan to complete this book.

**Ann with her husband Eldon
in the Hallie Stillwell Hall of Fame**

CPSIA information can be obtained at www.ICGtesting.com
Printed in the USA
BVOW10s1628131214

379262BV00002B/2/P